The Crossroads

Asking for the Ancient Paths

For the Glory of God in His Church!

Brett Heintzman

BRETT HEINTZMAN

This is what the LORD says: "Stand at the crossroads
and look; ask for the ancient paths, ask where the good
way is, and walk in it, and you will find rest for your souls.
But you said, 'We will not walk in it.'"

(Jeremiah 6:16 NIV)

WESTBOW°
PRESS
A DIVISION OF THOMAS NELSON
& ZONDERVAN

WestBow Press books may be ordered through booksellers or by contacting:

WestBow Press
A Division of Thomas Nelson & Zondervan
1663 Liberty Drive
Bloomington, IN 47403
www.westbowpress.com
1 (866) 928-1240

ISBN: 978-1-4908-6662-8 (sc)
ISBN: 978-1-4908-6664-2 (hc)
ISBN: 978-1-4908-6663-5 (e)

Library of Congress Control Number: 2015900693

Printed in the United States of America.

WestBow Press rev. date: 01/20/2015

Dedication

To my beloved family and colleagues in the Free Methodist Church: May the words contained in this writing inspire you to fully devoted service to our Lord and Savior Jesus Christ. Love Jesus deeply, seek Him earnestly, serve Him wholeheartedly, and may our hearts be undivided; turning completely away from the world and fixing our eyes on Jesus, the Author and Perfecter of our faith.

To my church family in Jamestown, NY. What shall I say? You are so dear to me and have taught me much. My life is rich and full because of you. Your love and devotion to Christ is evident. I humbly and gratefully thank our Lord for you always. You are a large part of this writing because you have been instrumental in my own faith journey. I love you deeply.

To my beloved Barb, who, with great patience has graciously allowed my retreats, struggles, and ponderings through this journey of life and has supported me through prayer and peace every step of the way. You have my heart now and always. We are one in this ministry.

To Jesus Christ, my all in all, my hope, joy and strength. To You, with God the Father and God the Holy Spirit, be all glory and praise now and forever, Amen.

Contents

Introduction

I recall the very first time I heard of a Free Methodist Church. I wondered what kind of church that could be? Having been raised in a Roman Catholic Church and then at age twelve in the Church of God (Anderson, IN), I had not the slightest notion of the Free Methodist Church or what distinguished it from any other Christian denomination. It would take many years, but I would later come to be a member of a Free Methodist Church (FMCUSA). However, even as I attended the church, I still did not come to know what distinguished it from every other Christian denomination. Only after I entered the path to ordained, pastoral ministry would I discover that the doctrine and life of holiness (i.e. entire sanctification) was the distinguishing gem at the heart of all Methodism and at the foundation of the Methodist view of the scriptures. The reason it took many years for me to discover the scriptural teachings on holiness? It was never taught or explained to me in the very church that claimed it as its distinctive doctrine. I like to say that holiness was, and is, hidden in plain sight.

Now, every time I hear "Free Methodist," I no longer wonder what kind of church that is. Instead I just wonder. I wonder what happened to lead us to the place where we no longer teach this scriptural truth. I wonder what would happen if we began to teach and proclaim holiness once again. I marvel in awe at the undeniable fact that Jesus intends to present to His Father a holy church. I wonder why so many of our pastors today don't preach holiness themes or principles. I wonder why our church today does not experience the power of God in the same ways as the early believers recorded in Acts.

It was in January of 2009 that Rev. Gerald Coates (then the Director of Communications for the FMCUSA) taught the course "History and Polity" for J-Term in Indianapolis. I was blessed to be one of his students. I went to this class to fulfill one of the many educational requirements for ordination, but I now believe God had me there on appointment. I wasn't sure what to expect at this class and thought perhaps it would be a dry presentation concerning policies and procedures. I hunkered down expecting a desert experience, but God showed up in a mountaintop-like way.

I thank God that Rev. Coates spent the majority of our class time together introducing us to a man named John Wesley. Yes, we studied Free Methodist discipline and polity, but I was captivated by the passionately devoted life of John Wesley and the beautiful ways that Rev. Coates revealed his heart to us through his journals and prayers. I saw in Wesley something missing in my own life: the burning desire to go after God and turn from everything in this world. It could be easily suggested that John Wesley's life had a singular purpose: *to serve Christ and His Kingdom*. I wanted that same devotion for myself. I wanted the same love for God and disdain for the world. I wanted the same passion for the lost. My heart was stirred, my spirit was electrified, my thoughts raced. I could clearly see that in Wesley was a complete and mature love for God: Father, Son and Holy Spirit, and a passion to see the Kingdom of God firmly established here on earth. Listen to the passionate determination in this quote:

> "Give me one hundred preachers who fear nothing but sin, and desire nothing but God, and I care not a straw whether they be clergymen or laymen; such alone will shake the gates of hell and set up the kingdom of heaven on Earth." – John Wesley

The more I learned of Wesley, the more I drew comparisons. I compared my own heart to his and I compared the Methodist revival of Wesley's day to the present condition of the Free Methodist Church. Back and forth my thoughts looked at *what was* and *what is*. I will admit that my views and understanding of our denomination were limited. Nevertheless, I drew parallels between my personal experience in my local church, and the heart, passion, and surrender in the life of Wesley. I drew parallels between the Methodist revival that transformed England and the relatively stagnant condition of the church of today. Things were not adding up for me. There was a fullness and power of the Holy Spirit in the Methodist reformation of the past that changed the course of a nation. I began to ask where that power was today. Had we embodied the undesirable quality of having "forms of religion" with no spiritual power? I performed a self-examination of my own life and recognized that my own church experience was all about events and programs rather than abiding in God's presence. I examined myself further and saw that I indeed suffered a shortage: a vacuum of God's power in my own life. I pondered how our own world today could be transformed if we, who call ourselves by the name Methodist, would embody Wesley's passion and desire. I pondered the ramifications of utter surrender to Christ, complete hatred of the things of the world, total devotion in service to Christ, and how that would change the course of *our* Church, *our* leaders, and join Christ in establishing His Kingdom here on earth.

At the conclusion of the class, Rev. Coates asked us if we had any questions or feedback. There was tension welling up in me created by the contradictions I sensed between what Wesley's experience had been, and the present condition of the church. The tension could remain penned up in my soul no longer. I raised my hand and said, "What I learned this week was that Wesley simply went after God with everything he had, and then, out of that, came the 'method.' When I look at all you've taught us, I wonder about the church today. I think if Wesley were here with us today he would kindly ask us to remove the word 'Methodist' from our church signs… or maybe not so kindly. How do we change things from where we are to return to what we've seen this week?" Rev. Coates smiled and reminded us that we were studying to be pastors, and that once called to serve a church, we would have the opportunity to lead in those ways.

In 2010, when I was called to serve a church as their pastor, I determined to do everything in my power not to waste the opportunity before me. My heart's desire was, and is, to embody the words of the Apostle Paul who said, "I want to know Christ and the power of his resurrection and the fellowship of sharing in his sufferings, becoming like him in his death." (Philippians 3:10) And I am determined to lead the people I serve to experience Christ in the very same way.

My personal journey with the Father, Son, and Holy Spirit has felt a bit like stepping onto a conveyor belt moving about 100 mph. The rate at which God has taught me, humbled me, changed me, corrected me, tested me and formed me has been quick, constant and intense. God has blessed me with a "great cloud of witnesses" who have fed me much like the ravens fed Elijah. (1Kings 17:4) I am blessed with the companionship of sojourners who love Jesus completely and who humbly and powerfully seek to see His Kingdom come on earth as it is in heaven. My life has become a story of death: death to self and death to the world.

Recently, I retreated with God at my beloved Free Methodist Camp at Cattaraugus, NY. God had called me away to that time with Him through the encouraging words of a sister who told me God was encouraging me to "hide thyself." Elijah heard these words from God and was called away into hiding in the ravine in Kirith, where he drank from the brook. (1Kings 17) I decided to obey God and unplug from the day-to-day rhythm of my life for ten days and listen for His voice.

On my first afternoon at the camp, God called me to the rear of the property at the top of a hill. As I neared the top, I could tell that there was a noticeable dip in the landscape so I continued to climb to see what it could be. I looked into this valley and saw an old abandoned set of railroad tracks.

The earth had once been blasted away and moved to make way for these tracks. They once carried trains, passengers, and goods of many kinds from one place to another. Now, the metal rails were gone, but the moss-covered, rotting remnants of the railroad ties were still present in the overgrowth. God spoke to me:

"The path has been abandoned, but the path is near.
Rebuild the old path."

Upon hearing those words, I wondered what they could mean. I like to figure things out right away, but God desired for those words to linger in my soul for a while first. After some time, the Holy Spirit began to reveal to me the meaning of His words. In the ten days I spent at the camp, God revealed His message for us as a church. Humbly, and with great respect for the church I love and serve, I am obediently responding to the Holy Spirit's call by giving you His message for us. This book is about recognizing the path we have abandoned but yet is very near to us. It is also about rebuilding the old path.

The old path to which we must return is the foundational path of holiness. Holiness transcends all cultures, all races, all generations, and all nations. Holiness is the heart condition that emerges from a life of death to self and pride. Holiness is not a doctrine to be studied or articulated, but a way of life, a path to walk. Holiness will change everything about a person who dies to self and lives into Christ.

The old path of holiness is not the old method of Wesley's day when God used class meetings and bands. Holiness in the people gave birth to their method, but the method was not holiness. The old path is not a legalistic list of dos and don'ts. When true holiness is found in us today, I'm convinced that God, who is both Creator and creative, will raise up fresh and life-giving expressions of that holiness to meet the spiritual challenges of our day. Therefore it is God we seek, God we die to, God we live into, and God we follow. As we seek God in and through holiness of life, He will guide us in the practical ways to serve Him in our communities. There is no substitute for this foundational work. We, in our humanity, roam off the tried and true path to other paths where we walk in the ingenuity of our own minds and the strength in our hands. We devise human plans and carry them out in the name of ministry. Though we honestly and sincerely seek to do good, we miss the very best. In the neglect of the old path, anything we attempt to build will be constructed on shifting sand. The Lord took me to these prophetic words He spoke through Jeremiah:

> This is what the LORD says: "Stand at the crossroads and look; ask for the ancient paths, ask where the good way is, and walk in it, and you will find rest for your souls. But you said, 'We will not walk in it.'" (Jeremiah 6:16)

The "crossroads", spoken of in this verse, is a point where decisions must be made, wrongs must be made right, repentance must occur, and a new direction must be considered. The crossroads represent a point where there is still time to change course and get on the right path. If the right path is taken, life and rest are promised.

Dear brothers and sisters in Christ, we stand at a crossroads. I say this in all sincerity, humility and love. The crossroads is at the intersection of apathy and action in regards to holiness and all of its implications for a rich and robust life in Christ. The following quote, taken directly from the website of Free Methodist World Missions, makes this statement:

> "The worldwide Free Methodist family includes more than 1 million members in 84 world areas. Only 7 percent of Free Methodists are in the United States."

Everywhere else in the world where the Free Methodist Church is located, it is growing faster than it is in the United States. With all of the resources, richness of history, and opportunities available to us, I question how this can be? Why do we not see the same explosive growth in the American Church that is being experienced underground in China or other creative access countries? In places around the world where American forms of religion are not allowed or not economically feasible, the power of God emerges in the day-to-day tangible ministry of the church. They have power without forms whereas we have forms without power. Because of this, it is time for us to sound a call and rediscover the old holiness path.

To reignite our passion, to join Christ in seeking and saving the lost, to acquire a deep burden for true revival, to turn the Holy Spirit loose in our lives and worship, to be dissatisfied with worldliness and seek true holiness: all these are within our grasp! We need not look any further than our own Wesleyan-Methodist heritage. Let us look not to the method but rather recapture the heart of Wesley who went after God with his whole heart, mind, soul and strength. This book is a call to a rebirth of the one and same passion that gave birth to Methodism.

We must heed the entire counsel of God found in Jeremiah's prophecy (Jeremiah 6:16) and stand, look, then ask. Standing indicates that we are attentive and ready for action. Looking indicates our willingness to keenly observe the current conditions and assess what needs to change. Finally, we must ask for the ancient paths and walk in them. When we have done all this, we will find rest for our souls and life in the church. As you read each chapter that follows, I suggest you use Jeremiah 6:16 as the lens through which you process these thoughts. Use Jeremiah 6:16 to observe and evaluate your own life as an individual, and the life of your church.

> "I will give them a heart to know me, that I am the
> LORD. They will be my people, and I will be their
> God, for they will return to me with all their heart."
> (Jeremiah 24:7)

I now invite you to join with me in taking up the heart and action of Wesley, who cried out to God with the psalmist saying, "Whom have I in heaven but you? And earth has nothing I desire besides you." (Psalms 73:25)

Amen.

CHAPTER ONE

Rebels

At the Crossroads of Apathy and Action.

A t the heart of who we are as a church lurks a spirit of rebellion. It's in our DNA.

Benjamin Titus Roberts, a Methodist Episcopal pastor serving God in upstate New York, became the founder of the Free Methodist Church. In 1852, B.T. Roberts was appointed to a church in Buffalo, NY. His mounting tension with the practices and spiritual powerlessness of the Methodist Episcopal Church brought him to a crossroads in his day. At issue was the battle between the God-given convictions that gripped his heart, and opposition to those convictions from within the church he served.

Roberts knew that it was not right to turn a blind eye to slavery. He knew that the "good seats" in the church should not be occupied only by those who had the financial means to pay a premium for them. He also knew that extravagant, performance-based worship had turned peoples' expectations to being entertained rather than sacrificing themselves in worship to God. He knew as well that holiness was nearing extinction, both in the lack of preaching and teaching from the pulpit and in the lack of evidentiary fruit in the lives of Methodists. He knew something had to be done.

Roberts' earnest attempt to bring reform to the Methodist Episcopal Church led him to act on his convictions. He was ultimately expelled from their ranks as an ordained minister due to his boisterous stand for what was right, just, godly, and holy. His failed attempts to be reconciled to the church in which he served left him and others no choice but to gather and worship in the context and proclamation of freedom.

Rebellion occurs when ideas, norms and/or practices accepted within a group are actively challenged. In terms of our Free Methodist history, we know this to be true. B.T Roberts asserted, and we still agree to, the following: Turning a blind eye to slavery... *wrong.* Charge money for seats in church ... *discriminates against the poor.* Highly formal worship ... *exclusive and unnecessary.* Holiness of life ... *Biblical and needed.* In the rising conflict there would either be reform or rebellion. After pressing and pushing on the Methodist Episcopal Church to condemn slavery, allow all seats in the church to be free, make worship simple, participatory and accessible, and preach holiness, the resulting resistance from the greater leadership within the Methodist Episcopal Church led to the holy rebellion that birthed the *Free* Methodist Church.

Rebellion gave birth to freedom. Once again, in the Free Methodist Church today there is need of rebellion leading to new freedom. The zealous and powerful condition of the Methodist Episcopal Church had changed from its inception in 1784 to the formal, powerless condition B.T. Roberts found and challenged in 1852-1858. In the same way, the Free Methodist Church that began in the latter part of 1860 has changed much during its history. Not all change for the Methodist Episcopal Church was *positive.* Hence the need for reform. In the same way, not all change for the Free Methodist Church has promoted true spiritual freedom. Hence the need for present-day reform.

Imagine what would have happened if B.T. saw the conditions of the church and simply decided to do nothing about it? One cannot rebel unless the erroneous norms have been identified. Had B.T. Roberts never assessed the situation and sounded the call to the people of his day, there would be no Free Methodist Church. History tells us, however, that B.T. Roberts *was* that calling voice to the Methodist Episcopal Church. The church chose to ignore the call.

Therefore, the looming question is, should a call be sounded today? Yes. I for one believe it is time to blow the trumpet and launch a rebellion in our beloved church. I believe it is time for an honest, soul-baring assessment of the current conditions. I believe our hearts need to be stung by the conviction of the Holy Spirit. I believe there are accepted norms to be challenged. However, the rebellion needed today is far different from that needed over 150 years ago.

Two sides of sin.

Most Christians subscribe to a one-sided view of sin. They believe that sin is the commission of an offense to God. This belief promotes the notion that if these offenses can be avoided, then we stand faultless before God, free of stain or blemish. Our thinking needs to be challenged. Actually, there are two sides to sin. They are:

1) To actively engage in the promotion and perpetuation of that which is defined as, and/or commanded to be unholy and evil by God.
2) To actively disengage from the promotion and perpetuation of that which is defined as, and/or commanded by God to be holy and good.

Do you see the difference and, yet, the similarity? Sin can manifest itself not only in the bad things we do, but also in the good things we neglect. To engage in evil is sin, and to disengage from holiness is sin. The first intends harm by its evil intent. The second does equal harm by its apathetic disengagement. James knew this as he wrote these words:

> "Anyone, then, who knows the good he ought to do
> and doesn't do it, sins." (James 4:17)

Jesus, through John, wrote the most telling letter to the church in Laodicea. We've all heard it before, but it bears repeating for the sake of the current discussion. It hits apathy at the center of its target.

> "To the angel of the church in Laodicea write: These are
> the words of the Amen, the faithful and true witness,
> the ruler of God's creation. I know your deeds, that
> you are neither cold nor hot. I wish you were either one
> or the other! So, because you are lukewarm—neither

hot nor cold—I am about to spit you out of my mouth. You say, 'I am rich; I have acquired wealth and do not need a thing.' But you do not realize that you are wretched, pitiful, poor, blind and naked. I counsel you to buy from me gold refined in the fire, so you can become rich; and white clothes to wear, so you can cover your shameful nakedness; and salve to put on your eyes, so you can see. Those whom I love I rebuke and discipline. So be earnest, and repent. Here I am! I stand at the door and knock. If anyone hears my voice and opens the door, I will come in and eat with him, and he with me. To him who overcomes, I will give the right to sit with me on my throne, just as I overcame and sat down with my Father on his throne. He who has an ear, let him hear what the Spirit says to the churches." (Revelation 3:14-22)

Just like the church in Laodicea, Jesus will call us to account if apathy has lulled us to sleep and if our ministry efforts are tepid and futile. We, too, will not escape the words of Jesus as He cross-examines our lives, looking for true spiritual fruit. He will call us out with the same indictment of being "wretched, pitiful, poor, blind and naked." His loving rebukes always shine a bright light on our soul-sick condition.

Apathy takes root when the good that should be done is neglected while a blind eye is turned to the bad that needs to be corrected. Apathy is at the heart of a "lukewarm church." We may know full well that change is needed and yet we blindly ignore the things that should be changed. No passion, no action, no change. We reason things away as being impossible to change or we transfer responsibility for the change to another party. We deceive ourselves, and here is the problem with deception: when a person (or church) is deceived, they are, in their own mind, convinced they are right but they are actually wrong... dead wrong! In the midst of deception people fight for what is wrong with great intensity and passion. Deception is at the core of apathy, and a corrective call must be sounded.

For Israel, God sounded this call through the Prophets.

> "Even now," declares the LORD, "return to me with all your heart, with fasting and weeping and mourning. Rend your heart and not your garments. Return to the LORD your God, for he is gracious and compassionate, slow to anger and abounding in love, and he relents from sending calamity. Who knows? He may turn and have pity and leave behind a blessing— grain offerings and drink offerings for the LORD your God. Blow the trumpet in Zion, declare a holy fast, call a sacred assembly." (Joel 2:12-15)

To escape the clutches of life-numbing apathy we must conduct an internal audit followed by engagement in an internal rebellion. Rebellion against self is the only way apathy can be put to death and have passion reawakened in the human heart. B.T. Roberts fought the same kind of foe. Roberts' passion to see apathy within the church awakened and corrected launched the rebellious call to change. We are descendants of that rebellion and we must now be willing to launch a fight against our own apathy.

Soul-baring examination.

> "Search me, O God, and know my heart; test me and know my anxious thoughts. See if there is any offensive way in me, and lead me in the way everlasting." (Psalms 139:23-24)

The psalmist had the right idea. Giving God permission to conduct an internal audit is regularly needed and always best. Recently

I led a prayer service where I sent everyone away with Psalm 139 for 30 minutes to ponder it and pray through its words. I instructed everyone to think and pray introspectively. That is, our praying was to focus on the singular relationship of ourselves and God, and we were to give God full permission to search us out and to speak to us personally. I, too, took part in praying the psalm. I was getting ready to preach for a family camp for 10 days and God had been giving me some messages of an intense nature. These messages, full of calls to deep devotion, heart-rending repentance and other similar topics, had churned up anxiety in my soul. I knew God had spoken but I feared repercussions from people. As I prayed, I openly asked God, "When you search me, what do You find?" God replied, "Brett, you don't trust Me." "How can you say that, God?" I replied. "You know I am committed to preaching all You have given me." "You are obedient," He said, "but your anxiety reveals a lack of trust." I knew it was true. I repented. God cleansed.

The question we must ask ourselves is this: Are we willing to consider for one moment that we might be wrong about the spiritual health of our churches and people? Could we be deceived into believing we are okay when we are lukewarm at best? This is where a very careful, self-aware examination must take place. We must take an honest and fearless look at our own hearts and the hearts of our churches. We must leave no door unopened, no closet untouched, no shelf undusted, no stone unturned. We must allow God to search us and reveal the findings.

This kind of examination requires a metric by which to measure. The measures must be those that are of the Kingdom of God, not of this world. Therefore we should not measure earthly things like buildings, budgets, attendance or dollars because they are not the best indicators of spiritual health. Truly, the first church grew daily without any of those things. In contrast, the following Kingdom measures look at the heart and the true spiritual fruit of the church. Bare your own soul and that of your church, allow God to speak, and honestly rate the following heart and fruit categories on the "Laodicean Scale."

Life Transformation *Displays of tangible life change into Christ-likeness.*	Cold ....Lukewarm................Hot
Redemption *People are healed and overcoming life's struggles.*	Cold ....Lukewarm................Hot
Help for the Poor and Disenfranchised *Passion and action combine to reach the poor with the* *Gospel regularly.*	Cold ....Lukewarm................Hot
Love *Unconditional, active love for the body and the world.*	Cold ....Lukewarm................Hot
Devotion to the Word of God *Passion to learn and obediently implement Jesus'* *commands.*	Cold ....Lukewarm................Hot
Spiritual Gifts *The body of Christ fully operates with every gift for the* *common good.*	Cold ....Lukewarm................Hot
New Spiritual Birth *Regularly witnessing new believers coming to faith.*	Cold ....Lukewarm................Hot
Social Change *The surrounding community is positively impacted with* *the good works of the church.*	Cold ....Lukewarm................Hot
Worship *Freedom in worship that allows the Holy Spirit to change* *human plans.*	Cold ....Lukewarm................Hot
Discipleship *People are taught to be submissive servants to our King.*	Cold ....Lukewarm................Hot
Engagement in Spiritual Battles *Fighting the spiritual war with spiritual weapons.*	Cold ....Lukewarm................Hot
Prayer *The necessity and love of prayer is evident as a priority.*	Cold ....Lukewarm................Hot
Generosity *People are inclined to selflessness in regards to their* *resources.*	Cold ....Lukewarm................Hot

The findings.

What did God reveal in your examination? What areas were cold, lukewarm and/or hot? The lukewarm areas are the places where apathy has settled in, where deception is blinding, and where Jesus will act in terms of expulsion. The fact that God will spew from His mouth anything lukewarm should indicate His displeasure with stagnation. We must become equally as disinterested and disgusted with lukewarm as He is. Ask Him to show you a glimpse of what He feels for all things lukewarm. With the truth of the findings before us, we find ourselves standing at the crossroads. In the standing we are aware, but awareness is not enough. We must act.

The new rebellion.

Therefore our own apathy, our own lack of holiness, our own coldness of love, our own neglect of the good, is what must be fought and defeated. If we desire to rise out of the ashes as holy, pure and powerful, we must be willing to launch an internal rebellion.

Launching an internal rebellion means we must seek the following:

- An awakening to our current condition.
- Repentance for neglecting the good we fail to do, as well as the offenses we commit.
- Passionately petition God to break our hearts for the lost, the poor, the prisoner, and the disenfranchised.
- An internal dissatisfaction with the status quo and our lukewarm areas.
- A yearning for personal and corporate holiness.
- A commitment to change.

No one would disagree with this list. It makes perfect sense, but it places us at the crossroads of apathy and action. Changing nothing means nothing changes. We must move, but in what direction? Can we continue in the slumber of lukewarm apathy? No. We will either move toward hot or cold, but it cannot be both and it cannot be neither. We must commit ourselves to an internal rebellion! It's time to awaken the spirit of rebellion that drove Wesley, Roberts and others to lead the church to revival and the resulting expansion of the Kingdom of God.

God is able to take dry, dead, lifeless, barren things and cause life to emerge from them.

> He asked me, "Son of man, can these bones live?" I said, "O Sovereign LORD, you alone know." Then he said to me, "Prophesy to these bones and say to them, 'Dry bones, hear the word of the LORD! This is what the Sovereign LORD says to these bones: I will make breath enter you, and you will come to life. I will attach tendons to you and make flesh come upon you and cover you with skin; I will put breath in you, and you will come to life. Then you will know that I am the LORD.'" (Ezekiel 37:3-6)

At some point in his life, having fought against the wrong he saw and losing his battle to reform the church that excluded him, B.T. Roberts' rebellion launched a freedom movement that has changed lives. His rebellion was an internal call for reform within the church. Today a new reform is needed. The old path of true holiness is needed. Soul-baring self-examination is needed. Honesty, repentance, humility and change are needed. As you approach the internal foe of self, will it succumb to change, or will it refuse?

Waiting on the other side of the internal rebellion is *freedom*.

CHAPTER TWO

Holiness

At the Crossroads of Self and Surrender

Consecrate: To set apart for a particular, singular purpose.
Sanctify: To set apart as holy, free from sin, sanctioned and dedicated to God.

Free Methodists are holiness people. The doctrine of entire sanctification or holiness is at the core of its history and experience. Yet recently, I have seen this doctrine widely debated, often misunderstood, and, at times, looked upon with suspicion or mystery. I've also sat in on conversations around this topic and discovered some reject the doctrine of entire sanctification altogether.

Why is this so? Is it for lack of biblical evidence? No, the scriptures clearly steer us away from sin and into God's holy presence, and the epistles instruct Christians to be holy people. Instead, it is likely due to a lack of both understanding and experience. Many brothers and sisters among us speak of sin as something that will always be with them. Others claim it is just too hard to squelch temptation. Is the power of sin greater than the power of the Holy Spirit? Has God left us helpless in our temptation, or has He identified in our weakness through Jesus and provided us a way out? Will we stand before God's throne of judgment one day and say, "You made me this way," expecting to be somehow excused for not "working out our salvation" with either holy fear or trembling? God has given us all the power we need to live holy lives, but our tendencies toward gratifying the flesh cause us to highly scrutinize the thought that we could actually be made *entirely* holy.

Another objection to entire sanctification is that it feels highly uncomfortable to imagine ourselves walking around through life announcing to the world that we have been completely made holy. The moment we label ourselves to be entirely sanctified opens us up to scrutiny by anyone who would stare into the glass house of our lives and see the real us.

These reasons, however, do not nullify the truth of sanctification. If holiness of life were dependent on human effort, one would most certainly fail. Perhaps we think that we have to earn this gift of God? No, there is indeed a part we play, but we are not the agent – you and I cannot do our own sanctifying work. Only God can. The one and only role we play in the process is to give entrance to the Great Renovator of souls. We must let God in and let God work. That's all.

Think of someone you know who is a great parent. How do you know that? Do they go around telling everyone who will listen to them that they are the best parent in town? Do they wear t-shirts announcing "I'm Mom of the Year!"? Certainly not. Your witness of their behavior signifies to you their dedication as a parent, as well as the results that spring forth in their children. It is the combination of inner dedication and outward evidence that tell you they are a devoted, good, solid parent.

All that being said, I am not inclined to enter the fray regarding any doctrinal debate on entire sanctification. Neither am I going to attempt to prescribe a formulaic approach to holiness by which you can experience Wesley's "strange warming" in your own heart. Instead, I desire to lead us to places of scriptural evidence pointing to the life of inward devotion and outward evidence that, together, signify a life of holiness.

We are standing at a critical crossroads where a choice must be made. Before a final decision is reached there will be a battle ... *a battle of wills*. God's will versus human will.

The one and only thing keeping any believer from a life of holiness is the failure to die to self.

So, with your indulgence, I'd like to tell you some of my life story. In the introduction I said, "My life has become a story of death; death to self and death to the world." Let me tell you how that came to be.

First love.

In the summer of 1978, my brother and I were outside playing in the front yard of our rural, Western New York home. A blue, Ford Econoline van stopped in front of our house. There were two people in the van and they asked if we were interested in coming to their church for VBS (Vacation Bible School). We took their flyer and asked our mom if we could go. She said, "Yes."

The van came back to take us each day. That week of VBS was the start of a completely new direction for my life and it all started with my teacher, Betty Swanson. Betty was a holy woman. I can say that now, though, at the time I met her I could have never figured out how to describe what seemed so genuine and different about her. Betty introduced me to Jesus. My life would never be the same, but not without many missteps along the way.

I fell in love with the church long before I fell in love with Jesus. By that, I mean that I loved the people because they were markedly different from the ways our highly dysfunctional family got along at home. I fell in love with the services because I loved music and the arts. The church actually provided a forum for my love of music to blossom. I fell in love with the activities and programs, dinners and fellowship, the people and the pastor. My pastor's wife, Judy, was especially kind and nurturing in my newness to the church and has left indelible imprints in my soul. As wonderful as all of that was, my love was first for the church. Yet Jesus was asking, "Brett, do you love Me?"

This love continued when I left Western New York for Florida in 1989. My dream had come true to serve in the capacity as a minister of music. This was an actual job doing what I really loved. I loved the job, I loved the music, and I loved the church. Yet Jesus was asking, "Brett, do you love Me?"

But things started to crumble. I married at the age of 25 not knowing that the relationship would one day end in divorce. I lacked maturity and depth and made many lousy choices. When I returned to New York in 1993, things had changed in the home church I loved so much. They had moved on without me and I felt quite out of place in the very place I loved so deeply. I was hoping to return to my first "church love." Yet Jesus was asking, "Brett, do you love Me?"

By the winter of 1994 I was lonely, unemployed, hurting and confused. In the spring of 1995 I was asked to help a church secretary in a Free Methodist Church with some computer training. I had acquired some skills with computers along the way and had been training people in software applications, so I decided to take the job. I sensed an opportunity for a fresh start. In fact, I know that God truly spoke to me during that season of my life. I believe it might have been the very first time God actually spoke directly through me. Just prior to Easter 1995, my wife and I began attending that church. I loved it… much like I had loved the other churches. Great music, an engaging pastor, nice people, a warm environment; this was my new church home. There was also an opportunity to use my musical gifts there. I loved Harvest Chapel Free Methodist Church. Yet Jesus was asking, "Brett, do you love Me?"

The next 15½ years saw church musical experiences I had only dreamed of. Once while I was in Florida, I attended a conference where a sixty-voice choir sang. I dreamed of directing such a choir. My dreams were realized at Harvest Chapel. Our choirs were inspiring. Our productions were as elaborate as one could expect for a small town and a church our size. People came from all around to experience these great pageants. I loved those days. I loved directing those choirs. Yet Jesus was asking, "Brett, do you love Me?"

One more musical dream came true for me. I, along with three close friends, formed a gospel quartet called "Soul Provider." We were enticed by some outside voices into believing we could "make it" in the gospel music business (whatever that means). We traveled and recorded a CD. As I stood in the recording studio in Nashville, TN, I thought I had died and went to heaven. I had "arrived." I loved our concerts, the recording process, and the accolades from people who followed us and loved our music. Yet Jesus was asking, "Brett, do you love Me?"

The coming crisis.

Mingled with the love of church and ministry was the looming succession of personal failures that would, once and for all, grab my attention and redirect my love to Jesus. My computer business (that I had seen as a gift of provision from God) was failing. My marriage (that I once thought to be solid) was toxic and crumbling. The various musical projects I loved began to lose their luster and seemed empty.

Ultimately, God would lead me to the place where I would forsake my "loves" to fall in love with Him. It would happen at my own crossroads of self and surrender. The last love to deal with was my ministry. A Pastoral transition had taken place at Harvest Chapel and things were being stirred within me. God was preparing the way.

At our church staff meeting one day, it seemed that the music from the previous Sunday was receiving large amounts of feedback of a critical nature. I wasn't accepting any of the comments very well. Following the meeting I had a conversation with the pastor. I said, "Music is the 'easy' thing for me. It's the thing I run to that usually gives me peace. Why is it feeling so 'hard', so 'uneasy?' Why is this a problem all of a sudden?" "You don't get it, do you?" my pastor replied. "No, I guess I don't. You're going to have to help me here." Then they said, "Jesus doesn't want you to run to *it*, He wants you to run to *Him*." I realized that my search for Jesus was always cluttered with church trappings and that I had never sought Him and Him alone, free of the add-ons. Jesus was asking, "Brett, do you love Me?"

Jesus calls us to surrender all to Him.

> If anyone comes to me and does not hate his father
> and mother, his wife and children, his brothers and
> sisters—yes, even his own life—he cannot be my
> disciple. And anyone who does not carry his cross
> and follow me cannot be my disciple. Suppose one
> of you wants to build a tower. Will he not first sit

down and estimate the cost to see if he has enough money to complete it? For if he lays the foundation and is not able to finish it, everyone who sees it will ridicule him, saying, "This fellow began to build and was not able to finish." Or suppose a king is about to go to war against another king. Will he not first sit down and consider whether he is able with ten thousand men to oppose the one coming against him with twenty thousand? If he is not able, he will send a delegation while the other is still a long way off and will ask for terms of peace. In the same way, any of you who does not give up everything he has cannot be my disciple. (Luke 14:26-33)

As Jesus started on his way, a man ran up to him and fell on his knees before him. "Good teacher," he asked, "what must I do to inherit eternal life?" "Why do you call me good?" Jesus answered. "No one is good— except God alone. You know the commandments: 'Do not murder, do not commit adultery, do not steal, do not give false testimony, do not defraud, honor your father and mother.'" "Teacher," he declared, "all these I have kept since I was a boy." Jesus looked at him and loved him. "One thing you lack," he said. "Go, sell everything you have and give to the poor, and you will have treasure in heaven. Then come, follow me." At this the man's face fell. He went away sad, because he had great wealth. (Mark 10:17-22)

A failed business, a failed marriage, and dissatisfaction in ministry. God was getting my attention. I was falling in love with Jesus, praying more than ever, loving His Word, and experiencing joy in the midst of my difficulties. Life was both bad and beautiful all together at the same time. I had fallen completely and entirely in love with Jesus. Jesus shows us the full extent of His love. The question remained for me: could I show Jesus the full extent of *my* love?

Three questions, three nails, and crucifixion.

In 2010, I was called to pastor the Free Methodist Church in Jamestown, NY. Answering the call to ministry was certainly a defining spiritual moment for me. However, a pinnacle moment was waiting on the horizon. It would cut much deeper, refine through a far hotter fire, and bring me as close to the kind of surrender Abraham was called to in sacrificing Isaac, as I would ever get.

God was guiding me to a place of challenge and asking me if I would allow His Spirit to have His way entirely in our worship. I confessed my hesitancy and apprehension even though I knew my answer must be, "Yes." God then asked me to surrender three things to Him. I believe God chose three questions for me that day just as Jesus asked Peter three times, "Do you love Me?" I too, just like Peter, was cut to the heart more with each question. These three questions contained the pain of the three nails driven into the hands and feet of Jesus. The death of my own will was about to take place.

God asked if was willing to give up my "things" to Him. This was the easiest of the three questions. Remember, at one time I had owned a business and two homes. Mind you, they were more modest than impressive, but the business failed, the finances failed, my marriage failed, and failure is failure no matter how you look at it. At that time, try as I might (with clenched fists), I simply couldn't retain any of those things. They all slipped away like sand flowing out from between my fingers, but I survived. I had not only survived, but God showed me a more excellent way. Living simpler has meant living freer so I had no trouble responding "Yes" to His first request. I laid my wallet and my checkbook (representing my resources), and my keys (representing the best of my belongings) on the table before me. I said, "Yes, Lord. If you asked me for these, they are Yours." The first question had been asked and the first nail driven.

God then presented the second request. "What if I asked you to surrender back to me your calling as a pastor?" With this request I was noticeably rocked. I love being a pastor. I love being a Free Methodist pastor, and I love where I pastor. My response took some careful thought and a bit more time. I was choked up. I said, "God, You were the One who called me. If You would ask me to surrender my calling, I am obligated to give it back to You, even though You are requesting the sacrifice of something I love deeply. But I have learned and know that I love you more." I opened my wallet that was on the table before me and removed my ministerial credentials. I laid the card on the table and placed the wallet back down as well. Tears were now coming into my eyes. "Yes, Lord. My calling I would give back to You." The second question had been asked and the second nail driven.

I thought there was nothing left until God asked the third question. His final request felt akin to the third nail driven into Jesus' feet, completing His crucifixion.

Before asking me His third request, God led me to this passage of scripture:

> The word of the LORD came to me: "Son of man, with one blow I am about to take away from you the delight of your eyes. Yet do not lament or weep or shed any tears. Groan quietly; do not mourn for the dead. Keep your turban fastened and your sandals on your feet; do not cover the lower part of your face or eat the customary food of mourners." So I spoke to the people in the morning, and in the evening my wife died. The next morning I did as I had been commanded. (Ezekiel 24:15-18)

I was just recently married to my beautiful wife Barb. I began to shake and my hands were quivering. I was sobbing and said, "Lord, surely You're not asking me what You asked of Your servant, Ezekiel?" "What if I was?" God replied. "Would you surrender Barb to Me if I asked you to?" I knew deep within that God *could* do whatever He chose in my life and that surrender was the only way; my only option. I cried and fought the urge but I soon removed my wedding band from my hand. As I looked at it, I was remembering the night we bought our rings. I had experienced a euphoric love I thought I'd never find again on earth. Now I was gripped with an unknown and unexpected grief at the thought that God would actually do what was being suggested. I slowly placed my ring on the table with the other objects. My wallet, keys, checkbook, ministerial credentials and now my wedding band were on the table before me. Outside of my own flesh and blood, nothing else remained. I was bare and broken. "Yes, Lord, even Barb." I sobbed these words out almost unintelligibly.

"Thank you for giving them to Me," God said. "You may now pick them back up."

My life was handed back to me, yet I had died. I was crucified with Christ and yet I was still living. At my own crossroads of self and surrender, I walked the ancient path of surrender. In the wake of utter surrender my human will was broken, allowing only room for God's will. I'm more confident I can answer Him with my "Yes" and "Amen" no matter what He asks. My first and only true love has been fixed on Jesus.

The one and only thing keeping any believer from a life of holiness is the failure to die to self.

The death that comes before death.

When Jesus looks at us He sees something worth dying for.

When we look at Jesus, do we see something worth dying for?

Do the scriptures support this idea of "death to self?" Yes, indeed they do. Consider the following passages:

> "I have been <u>crucified</u> with Christ and I <u>no longer live</u>, but Christ lives in me. The life I live in the body,

I live by faith in the Son of God, who loved me and gave himself for me." (Galatians 2:20)

Peter answered him, "<u>We have left everything</u> to follow you! What then will there be for us?" (Matthew 19:27)

Then God said, "Take your son, your only son, Isaac, whom you love, and go to the region of Moriah. <u>Sacrifice him there</u> as a burnt offering on one of the mountains I will tell you about." (Genesis 22:2)

Then Paul answered, "Why are you weeping and breaking my heart? <u>I am ready not only to be bound, but also to die</u> in Jerusalem for the name of the Lord Jesus." (Acts 21:13)

The inner rebellion will either prevail or suffer defeat at the crossroads of self and surrender. Those who choose surrender over self die in advance of their death. Paul was able to say he was "crucified with Christ" because he chose surrender over self. Peter acknowledged that he had left everything to follow Jesus because surrender won out over self. Abraham took Isaac and fully intended to sacrifice him because he was on the path of surrender. Paul verified his surrender when he said, "I am ready not only to be bound, but also to die in Jerusalem for the name of the Lord Jesus." (Acts 21:13) Even though it took me a long time to arrive at the place of death in my own life, God proved this truth of entire sanctification to me in two ways. First, through the scriptures, so I could know about sanctification in my mind, and then through my personal experience as I surrendered all to Him and subjected my will to His.

For the longest time, I never understood what must go through the mind of someone who is martyred for the sake of Christ. I can recall youth group meetings as a teenager where a mock-hijacking would occur and people would storm into the room demanding that we renounce our faith in Christ or die. We were all familiar with the drill. We knew the correct answer but it was a set-up, not real life. But what if our lives were threatened simply because we knew Jesus? I believe that no human is capable of the martyr's response without first dying in advance of their physical death.

Dead to the world and alive in Christ. Dead to self and surrendered to God's will and ways. That is the essence of holiness, and holiness is needed now more than ever.

> Do not love the world or anything in the world. If anyone loves the world, the love of the Father is not in him. For everything in the world—the cravings of sinful man, the lust of his eyes and the boasting of what he has and does—comes not from the Father but from the world. The world and its desires pass away, but the man who does the will of God lives forever. (1 John 2:15-17)

It is this amazing combination of inner devotion and death, alongside the outward supporting evidence, all done through the power and inner working of the Holy Spirit, that produces holiness in unholy flesh. Is this possible? Is it possible to be "entirely sanctified?" Based on the biblical accounts and the power of God, I will answer with a confident, "Yes." Will I roam this earth telling anyone who will listen that I am entirely sanctified? I will refuse to use those words. Rather, I'll allow my inner devotion to remain dead to self before my God, and allow Him to be alive in every outward deed of my life, to do the speaking. And should anyone see holiness in me, may all the glory, honor and praise go to God the Father, who gave us Jesus, His Son, and sent the powerful Holy Spirit.

A church without holiness?

Is it possible to have a church without holiness? Perhaps if we are studying literal definitions of the word *church*, we would have to say, "No." Perhaps the question should be rephrased. Is it possible for a group of people to claim to be a church and do churchy things without holiness? Yes, absolutely! When a person or group of people claims to be part of a holy church and has neither the inner devotion and death, nor the outward fruit, the damage that is caused is beyond troubling.

In the year 1879, author J.C. Ryle penned these words: "Sound Protestant and Evangelical doctrine is useless — if it is not accompanied by a holy life. It is worse than useless; it does positive harm. It is despised by keen-sighted and shrewd men of the world, as an unreal and hollow thing, and brings religion into contempt."[1]

Verbal Christian professions of faith that are not supported and evidenced by holy living do "positive harm." This statement is beyond true. This statement speaks to the foundational truth behind every comment ever uttered claiming the church is full of hypocrites. Wherever our actions do not align perfectly with our words, we become hypocrites. When we speak of holiness and our lives do not show the inward devotion or outward evidence of the Spirit's presence, we are agents of "positive harm." For this reason, holiness of life, surrender to Christ, continual growth in knowledge and grace, and an urgency from the pulpit to align our actions with our words is vital.

The one and only thing keeping any church from a life of holiness is the failure of the pastor to die to self.

---

[1]   Booth, William ; Wesley, John ; Bonar, Horatius; Ryle, J. C. ; Brengle, Samuel; Taylor, Jeremy; Law, William (2012-02-27). Top 7 Classics on Holiness: Purity of Heart, Heart Talks on Holiness, Holiness, God's Way of Holiness, Christian Perfection, Serious Call, Holy Living (Top Christian Classics) (Kindle Locations 2465-2467). Kindle Edition.

A Pastor's power is found in a life of walking the ancient path of personal holiness.

Fellow Pastors and colleagues: can you and I, along with Peter, say to Jesus, "We have left everything to follow You"? Have you passed by the crossroads of self and surrender and chosen the holy way of surrender? Have you abandoned self to walk the holy path of surrender, or have you abandoned the holy path of surrender to walk in your own ways?

Church organizations can be run by talented and clever men and women using their human strength and ingenuity to do a lot of "ministry." Think about it. Charitable organizations, businesses, civic clubs, and groups of many different kinds do creative things every day. They use human creativity and ingenuity to promote and lead their people. Creative, passionate, talented leaders can do good things for a good organization. Churches, however are supposed to be entirely "other." The church simply cannot be the church without holiness. It is the inward devotion and outward fruit signifying that the Kingdom of God is at hand. And the church has no hope of rising into her distinct identity without holiness in its pastors.

When the spies returned from Canaan with the report of what was found in the land God had promised to the people of Israel, they spread a bad report. The people grumbled against Moses and Aaron. Two of the spies, Joshua and Caleb, tore their clothes because they were so distraught. In the midst of this conflict, Moses and Aaron speak:

> "If the LORD is pleased with us, he will lead us into that land, a land flowing with milk and honey, and will give it to us. Only do not rebel against the LORD. And do not be afraid of the people of the land, because we will swallow them up. Their protection is gone, but the LORD is with us. Do not be afraid of them." (Numbers 14:8-9)

"Is the Lord pleased with us?" "Do not rebel against the LORD." "We will swallow up the enemy." "The LORD is with us." "Do not be afraid." These are pastoral words that lead people out of their fears and into holy confidence. As pastors, we are no different today.

Pastors and leaders: can we expect to teach our people how to navigate the crossroads of self and surrender, and emerge victorious over self and sin, if we have never victoriously navigated it ourselves? We who lead the church must be fully surrendered. We must be dead to this world and alive in Christ. We must be sold as slaves to righteousness and also entirely sanctified if we would hope to see our people live into the high and holy calling that Jesus gives to all who join Him in His death and life. This message of surrender must be the rhythm of your own sacrificial life.

> "We always carry around in our body the death of Jesus, so that the life of Jesus may also be revealed in our body." (2 Corinthians 4:10)

In addition, does your congregation know your "surrender story"? Have you, by your own transparency, led people through their own crossroads of self and surrender? Is your love for God in its rightful first place? Do your people know how God continues to be at work in your life? Are you open, honest and real? Are you willing to set the tone so that they, too, can be open and honest about where they are on the path?

How well cared-for is your own intimate relationship with God?

> "Abide in Me, and I in you. As the branch cannot bear fruit of itself, unless it abides in the vine, neither can you, unless you abide in Me. I am the vine, you are the branches. He who abides in Me, and I in him, bears much fruit; for without Me you can do nothing." (John 15:4-5 NKJV)

To effectively minister we must abide in the Vine, Jesus. Apart from Him all our ministry efforts will not produce fruit for the Kingdom. Abiding in Jesus maintains the rhythm of daily surrender to Christ, ensures His voice is regularly speaking into our life, and keeps us in a place of soul-baring accountability before God on a regular basis. Abiding in Jesus takes time that is not shared with any other activity or task. Abiding can't be rushed and can't be manufactured.

If this Vine-abiding life is the key to pastoral leadership and if we expect to see it emerge in the lives of those we serve and lead, then it must also emerge from our preaching.

Holiness preaching empowers people. Pastors, preach the ancient path of holiness.

God's message of living a holy life of death through surrender and abiding in Christ should be the underlying theme of every message preached.

The reason I say this with such certainty is that most people, pastors included, are living earthly lives under a new role, serving a new King. We are earthly workers, parents, children, husbands, wives, bosses, and laborers all journeying the everyday through a holy worldview. We don't see earth, we see the merger of heaven and earth. We don't live under the bondage of sin but we stand next to those who do every single day. Holiness is needed in the world today, and only the church can supply that need. If holiness is not addressed in the messages with which we encourage and exhort our people, then there is likely going to be little impact in the sinful world around them. Yes, holiness must be preached because holiness matters in an unholy world.

> "How, then, can they call on the one they have not
> believed in? And how can they believe in the one

of whom they have not heard? And how can they
hear without someone preaching to them?" (Romans
10:14)

I had the privilege of taking one of my required classes for
ordination under the teaching of Dr. Michael Walters, Associate
Dean for Biblical Studies, Theology and Philosophy at Houghton
College. On the first day of class, Dr. Walters said this, "Today, most
churches are elementary schools for moral education." That phrase
has stuck with me, and will likely remain in my mind for life. It has
also shaped my thoughts, my preaching and my teaching regarding
holiness as God's plan and God's call to all who would be His disciples.
Holiness preaching is designed to bring people to the crossroads of
self and surrender, the root issue of all of life's experiences.

Preaching morals and practicalities will help people survive
life. Self-help groups help people survive life's difficulties every
day. Preaching holiness will produce disciples who are "more than
conquerors." Preaching morals and practicalities aims at *behavioral
change*. Preaching holiness aims at *spiritual transformation*. Preaching
holiness leads people to the "sudden death" moments of life in Christ
in ways that relate to their every-day issues. Preaching holiness leads
people to the crisis moment before God where all is surrendered.
Preaching holiness teaches both eternal life, and the route through
death that must take place to inherit that eternal life.

Encourage and teach in the direction of a fully-surrendered life,
deeply devoted to God inwardly, and outwardly bearing the fruit of
the Spirit; this is the life and evidence of holiness. Preach it. Live it.

The death of the church.

The one and only thing keeping the Free Methodist Church or
any church from holiness and kingdom expansion is the failure to
die to itself.

Why do we complicate things by creating organizations?

I direct a men's a cappella barbershop chorus. It's both a pastime and a place to ask for God's Kingdom to come to earth through ministry. On April 11, 1938, two men, along with numerous invited guests, got together on the rooftop garden of the Tulsa Club in Tulsa, Oklahoma to sing some old four-part barbershop songs. These men could have never imagined what kind of blaze their spark would produce. The popularity of this nearly lost art form called barbershop quartet singing was revived from near extinction and began spreading at light speed. In response to the growth and popularity, the people involved did what people do… they created an organization.

Fast forward.

This organization now has nationwide districts, worldwide affiliate organizations, directors, presidents, vice presidents of many varying degrees, chapters in every corner of the country with multiple officers and directors in each chapter, dues that need to be paid, membership cards, programs and plans, a website, marketing tools, promotional products, and music schools. My goodness, the list is nearly exhausting. All of this organizing centered around two men who thought, "Wouldn't it be great to get some friends together and sing some old barbershop songs?"

And there's more: competitions with rules and regulations. Judges who need to be certified to score the competitions, and even rules to dictate what type of songs are allowable in competition. There are trophies and awards… formality and protocol… are you getting the point?

I once went to a District Officer's Training event. We spent two whole days learning about how leadership within our organization is *done*. Guess what? Not one song was sung the entire weekend. What a disappointment! What a wake-up call!

If the purpose of a barbershop chorus is to make music but it stops making music because it spends so much time on its structures and organizational details, it has lost its way and no longer serves its intended purpose. Let's apply this principle to our churches. The purpose of the church is to love God, love people, make disciples as Jesus did, and to set up the Kingdom of God on earth by preaching and demonstrating the power of the Kingdom. If we abandon this holy purpose for the sake of managing the organizational trappings we have constructed around the church, then we have lost our way and no longer serve the world, but serve only ourselves.

The "Kingdom song" of holiness must be "sung" in God's Church.

A rebellion should be launched against our apathy toward holiness when our passion is misdirected to the business of *doing church*. This can only be accomplished by putting to death our deception that "organizational activity" is equivalent to Kingdom productivity. Remember, apathy occurs when we actively disengage from the promotion and perpetuation of that which is defined as holy and good by God. Let us not neglect the good that can blossom from living holy lives, preaching holiness, and demonstrating holiness in every area of our lives by over-feeding the organizational constructs we have built for ourselves. Board meetings, offices and officers, programs and procedures are pointless if they do not serve God's true purposes.

In the Free Methodist Church, our leadership and organizational structures can give the impression that leadership is a "top-down" model. Churches look to their pastors who, in turn, look to their District Leaders, Superintendents and Bishops. However, we all serve the King of all kings and therefore everything serves Christ and His Kingdom. With Jesus as King and Head of His Church, all our organization must be subjected to the bottom of the food chain: serving Jesus from the bottom up, not the top down. Therefore, just as individuals must subject their will to Christ through surrender, so too must our churches subject their will to Christ by surrendering organization for the beauty of His mission.

A holy prayer of surrender.

When Jesus' disciples asked Him to teach them to pray, Jesus gave them these words:

> "This, then, is how you should pray: "'Our Father in heaven, hallowed be your name, your kingdom come, your will be done on earth as it is in heaven. Give us today our daily bread. Forgive us our debts, as we also have forgiven our debtors. And lead us not into temptation, but deliver us from the evil one.' (Matthew 6:9-13)

Using Christ's words, let's turn them into a personal prayer for both individuals and churches. The Lord's Prayer is a prayer of holiness and surrender. It acknowledges God as our Father, Provider, Sustainer and Savior. This prayer places us before God, confessing our need for His holiness and generous provision. Use this prayer to subject your own will to God's will. Finally, to ensure God's Kingdom purposes are fully accomplished in and through our churches, and to ensure they remain our first priority, this prayer applies to the greater church, its leaders and organizational structures.

Our Father in heaven, hallowed be your name.

> Our Father, your name is holy and is to be revered. May we live in awe of You and seek to live into and honor Your holiness. Lord God, may we as individuals, and may our pastors, churches and all leaders continually remain in complete subjection to, and service to, You as King of all kings and Lord of all lords.

Your kingdom come, your will be done on earth as it is in heaven.

> We are lost if Your Kingdom does not come in and through us. May it be always true that Your Kingdom purposes remain our only goal and our first priority, both for us as individuals and for the greater church.

Give us today our daily bread.

> May we never look to ourselves as the source of our supply. We trust you for Your provision. Our churches trust You for provision. Just for today, show us all how to serve You best by serving one another in Your church. Keep us on our knees, daily trusting You to provide.

Forgive us our debts, as we also have forgiven our debtors.

> Forgive us, Lord if we have ever served ourselves or betrayed Your holy trust in any ways of disservice to Your church. We repent. We also forgive and must remain ready to forgive any other harm done to us.

And lead us not into temptation, but deliver us from the evil one.

> Let us never be tempted to elevate the names or titles of churches, leaders, or denominational constructs above the name of Jesus, the Name above every name. May we never be tempted to bow our knee to our own "kings" and may we flee all temptation toward pride for any victories or accomplishments. Keep us pure, white and holy in Your Presence.

For Thine is the Kingdom, the power, and the glory forever.

> The church is not ours, it is Yours. We are dust if we are not Your Kingdom. Your blood bought us and we are not our own. We are only free because you purchased our freedom. We have no methods unless You tell us Your plans. We are Yours forever because You are eternal.

Amen.

> Let it be so as long as we have the honor of serving You as a church.

Individuals, pastors, leaders, churches and entire denominations must die to self and live into Christ. We must abide in the Vine and He in us. With every act of surrender to God we are more and more consecrated to the singular purpose of serving Christ in His Kingdom as His disciples. Let us truly live our lives fully consecrated and entirely sanctified to that one, holy singular purpose.

Holiness. It is the ancient path we must ask for at the crossroads of self and surrender. At the crossroads our ways must be considered and a choice must be made. Will your will or God's will be done?

> For it is written: "Be holy, because I am holy."
> (1 Peter 1:16)

CHAPTER THREE

The Holy Spirit

At the Crossroads of Cooperation and Control

37

Without the Holy Spirit, there is no holiness. Without His power, there is no victory. Without His leading, we have no worthwhile plans. Without His presence, we are left as desolate orphans.

The crossroads before us, in regards to the power and presence of the Holy Spirit, is the intersection of cooperation and control. We will either cooperate with the Holy Spirit, or we will insist on having our own way. Jesus described the two roads from which people may choose to travel.

> "Enter through the narrow gate. For wide is the gate and broad is the road that leads to destruction, and many enter through it. But small is the gate and narrow the road that leads to life, and only a few find it." (Matthew 7:13-14)

There is a narrow road that leads to life. That narrow road is the way of holiness. It is where both individuals and churches cooperate fully with the voice and leading of the Holy Spirit. The wide road is the way of self. It is where both individuals and churches retain control and insist on having their own way. The narrow road can feel a bit risky, so only a few find it. The wide road is comfortable and familiar. The wide road has far fewer chances for experiencing true faith, but it's predictable. The narrow road requires surrender and careful attentiveness to the voice of God. The wide road is full of forms of religion with no power where we retain control over our lives. Only one road can be traveled. Will we cooperate with the Holy Spirit to have His way, or will insist on control? If you are on the narrow road of holiness, it will be visible through the power and presence of the Holy Spirit.

Businesses distinguish themselves from competitors by finding niche markets or using creative marketing ploys. Charitable organizations distinguish themselves by championing a cause, filling a need, or righting a wrong. However, what distinguishes the church from any other people group in the world is the power and the presence of the Holy Spirit. In fact, it is impossible to produce fruit that is authentically spiritual without the power and presence of the Holy Spirit.

The distinctive of the church is the manifestation and demonstration of the Holy Spirit's power that accompanies the proclamation of the Good News of the Kingdom of God. That alone is what sets us apart. As Free Methodists, our doctrinal teaching of entire sanctification has no power, no effect, no validity, no "teeth" without the power and presence of the Holy Spirit. When the Holy Spirit, through surrender of a person's will, is given full access to that person's life, the Spirit's power and presence will inevitably and quite naturally lead to a life of personal holiness: entire sanctification in all its fullness.

Paul describes how the Holy Spirit's power and presence was foundational in his ministry.

> When I came to you, brothers, I did not come with eloquence or superior wisdom as I proclaimed to you the testimony about God. For I resolved to know nothing while I was with you except Jesus Christ and him crucified. I came to you in weakness and fear, and with much trembling. My message and my preaching were not with wise and persuasive words, but with a demonstration of the Spirit's power, so that your faith might not rest on men's wisdom, but on God's power. (1 Corinthians 2:1-5)

The prophet Joel foretold, and Jesus confirmed, the coming of the Holy Spirit.

> And afterward, I will pour out my Spirit on all people. Your sons and daughters will prophesy, your old men will dream dreams, your young men will see visions. Even on my servants, both men and women, I will pour out my Spirit in those days. I will show wonders in the heavens and on the earth, blood and fire and billows of smoke. The sun will be turned to darkness and the moon to blood before the coming of the great and dreadful day of the LORD." (Joel 2:28-31)

But I tell you the truth: It is for your good that I am going away. Unless I go away, the Counselor will not come to you; but if I go, I will send him to you. (John 16:7)

We must never be deceived into thinking that forms of worship or rightly articulated doctrine is equivalent to holiness of life birthed through the power and presence of the Holy Spirit. In other words, participation in a worship service is not necessarily a demonstration of the Holy Spirit's power, and the recitation of doctrine does not necessarily indicate the Holy Spirit's presence. Jesus told the Pharisees and the Teachers of the Law that though they studied the law and adhered to every edict it contained, their father was the devil. (John 8:44) Furthermore, Stephen, prior to his stoning and filled with the Holy Spirit, told the Sanhedrin they always resisted the Holy Spirit. (Acts 7:51) To walk humbly before God is to be ever mindful that there might be something of which we may need to repent.

Addressing the present hunger.

God is welling up a hunger in the hearts of Christians everywhere for the fullness of the Holy Spirit. Whenever I have the occasion to preach about the power and presence of the Holy Spirit, I find that hungry people come out of their hiding places to talk with me. These people have experiences of seeing into the spiritual realm. They engage in spiritual warfare. Many have the gift of praying in the Spirit (tongues). Others are overwhelmed with emotions of various kinds when the Holy Spirit comes upon them. At times, they feel oppressed in worship. They feel if they were as expressive or emotional as they desired, they would surely be misunderstood or even chastised by church authorities.

These brothers and sisters are misunderstood, and therefore criticized, for the particular manifestation(s) of the Spirit's power God has given them; the misunderstanding comes from others within the church. People intentionally stuff their gifts to avoid being open to public criticism. I spoke to one dear sister who loves her local church, yet chooses to conduct prayer meetings in her home because she, and the others in the prayer meeting, desire to be fully Spirit-led, and fear that the ways in which the Holy Spirit manifests Himself would be unwelcome in their own church. In these meetings, people prophesy and pray in tongues. People pray the scriptures and hear words of knowledge given to them by God for the building up of others. God maintains order as His Spirit moves and guides these meetings, sometimes for hours.

These friends I speak of, though nameless, are actual people with real stories. They are present in the Church *right now*. Because I encounter these dear people wherever I have the opportunity to speak about the power and presence of the Holy Spirit, I can safely assume they are not alone.

Allow me to ask this question: Why must they hide or risk criticism?

Sadly, the answer may be that we seek to control our churches to hold to specific forms rather than act in cooperation with the Holy Spirit. Truth be told, we are most comfortable with "those people" through whom the Holy Spirit is manifest in certain ways, doing what they do on their own time in the privacy of their own homes. We would rather not welcome them (and their gifts) within the constructs of Sunday morning worship.

We should be asking if something is lacking, not in terms of tangible, earthly things, but in terms of the Spirit's demonstrative power. Could it be that the spiritual lack could explain the spiritual decline in so many churches? Is your church struggling to make a real spiritual impact in your community? Better and more complicated structures within your church do not equate to spiritual impact in the world around you. Only deep spirituality will address the deep spiritual deficit both within the church and in the world.

We've all heard of churches that suffer conflict over opposing parties seeking to control the church. This type of war within churches always causes harm and destruction while weakening our witness to the world. No good can come from squabbles over control of the church. Surrender to the Holy Spirit is the only and best answer. Holiness is the key. Holy and surrendered people will seek resolutions to conflicts but never demand to control. Is there an issue with control in your church? Holiness will solve it.

God is asking us to accept Him on His own terms. God is asking us to repent of the limitations we have placed on His movement through human management and control. God is asking us to throw open the floodgates of our own souls to allow Him to move in all His beauty and fullness.

Here we stand at the crossroads of cooperation and control. What will we do? Have we considered the price we will pay if we choose control?

The Church is, above all, spiritual.

Ask for the ancient path of true spirituality and true spiritual worship.

> "God is spirit, and his worshipers must worship in spirit and in truth." (John 4:24)

"...but God has revealed it to us by his Spirit. The Spirit searches all things, even the deep things of God. For who among men knows the thoughts of a man except the man's spirit within him? In the same way no one knows the thoughts of God except the Spirit of God. We have not received the spirit of the world but the Spirit who is from God, that we may understand what God has freely given us. This is what we speak, not in words taught us by human wisdom but in words taught by the Spirit, expressing spiritual truths in spiritual words. The man without the Spirit does not accept the things that come from the Spirit of God, for they are foolishness to him, and he cannot understand them, because they are spiritually discerned." (1 Corinthians 2:10-14)

No student of the Bible nor any reasonable child of God would deny this seemingly elementary fact as being completely true: that the church is, above all, spiritual. To merely say the church is spiritual is true, but it begs the question: Do our actions, expectations, and behaviors align themselves with our words? Alongside our proclamation that the church is spiritual, we must encounter and accept that the church is equally supernatural. We cannot have spirituality without supernatural power; the two are inseparable. To believe God, to believe in Jesus and that God raised Him from the dead, to believe in the bodily resurrection from the dead, and to accept all these things by faith, justifying us before God who is Spirit, requires that we all, at some level, acknowledge and affirm the spiritual and the supernatural nature of the church. It takes supernatural power to heal, to part the Red Sea, and to raise the dead. It takes supernatural power to perform signs and wonders in the name of Jesus. To see demons flee at the name of Jesus demands our affirmation of the supernatural.

As we speak about our faith, it is rare that our words alone would contradict biblical truths or principles. Many have learned well from the massive amounts of Christian education opportunities afforded them how to articulate what they believe. However, it is usually our actions that fail to line up with what so easily passes by our lips. Words reflect head knowledge drawn from the scriptural accounts, but demonstrations of the Spirit's power require that the spiritual, supernatural power of God be involved. You see, I contend that there should and must be manifestations of the Spirit's power and presence in the day-to-day life and worship of a body of believers if we are the holiness people we say we are.

I believe we can all affirm the following:

- We serve a God who is Spirit.
- His Kingdom is spiritual.
- His gifts are spiritual.
- His enemies are spiritual.
- The weapons with which we fight the enemy are spiritual.
- The power we are given is spiritual.
- Church leaders and the leadership they offer must be spiritual.
- Our prayer must be spiritual.
- Our expectations must be for the supernatural.

It's all about His presence.

Ask for the ancient path of abiding in His presence.

I have a pastor-friend in Monroe, Michigan named John Piippo. I call him a friend although we don't have a close personal relationship. The reason I call him friend is because I resonate so closely with his heart and passion for what he calls the "presence-driven church." John asserts that what drives the church he serves is not programs or even purposes but the power and presence of the Holy Spirit. He cites the following passage from Exodus:

> The LORD replied, "My Presence will go with you, and I will give you rest." Then Moses said to him, "If your Presence does not go with us, do not send us up from here. How will anyone know that you are pleased with me and with your people unless you go with us? What else will distinguish me and your people from all the other people on the face of the earth?" (Exodus 33:14-16)

Being driven by the very presence of God in all we do as a church affirms the spirituality and supernatural qualities of the church. To be preference-driven, program-driven, or even purpose-driven falls short of the design that God be in full control of His church. I, as a pastor, am to lead but not manipulate; guide, but never control; steward, but not manage Christ's church for which He died. To be presence-driven is to move from the scriptural/doctrinal to the spiritual/supernatural; from the power found in the biblical story to experiential power in our own story; from what is bound and loosed in heaven to binding and loosing on earth; from mere belief to *active belief*. And all of this should be submitted to the desires, directives and dictates of the Spirit.

Expectantly seeking His presence.

Ask for the ancient path of expectant faith.

As the pastor of my church, I'm the primary person charged with leading and guiding weekly worship services. When it comes to planning for a weekly worship service, I engage in all the typical activities that lead to the planning and preparations necessary to pull off a worship service. I pray and study, write a message, and check with my worship leader to see what songs have been selected. I ensure that a bulletin is printed and everything is in its place. I am pretty good at planning and preparation for programs and services; I have been planning programs most of my life, so I'm always prepared for the congregation to arrive on Sunday mornings.

And then there's the average church attender. As a member of a local church, do you come to church with something to give (monetary offerings are not the emphasis here), or do you come to church prepared to receive what has been prepared on your behalf. Is your church service a predictable event or free to move as the Holy Spirit leads?

There is nothing more life-giving than living in the presence of our Holy God as His people gather to worship Him! When God has interrupted our plans and asked for something different, we step to one side and allow Him full entrance.

One Sunday in late January 2011, I entered the morning worship having wrestled with the passage of scripture found in Matthew 5:31-32 where Jesus speaks about divorce. I knew the day would come when God would ask me to preach on this passage because my first marriage ended in divorce. When I accepted my call, I told God that I must be willing to preach on that topic or I would be of no use to Him. What kind of Pastor would I be if I could not preach the truth from the entire consult of scripture, regardless of my own sin and shortcomings? I obediently, albeit not too confidently, entered the Sanctuary that morning prepared to deliver His message. God had different plans. The morning took on a new life and God had me preach on prayer that morning. The Holy Spirit thanked me for being willing to enter the wrestling match with Him over that passage of scripture and then released me from having to preach it. Worship was glorious that morning. God taught me about redemption and showed me the way to preach concerning sin from my own experience. By the way, God did have me preach the message on divorce at a later time and I preached it both obediently and confidently.

The Holy Spirit will lead us into and through His power and presence if we will allow Him the role of Leader. When we willingly surrender control, He takes the lead. When we insist on control, He withdraws and steps aside.

On another occasion, our worship took a Spirit-led turn toward a beautiful, cleansing time of prayer. An African-American gentleman was testifying in the service about how he had been searching for a job. His language was full of innuendo that led me to discern he was experiencing racial oppression. He would speak of each lost job opportunity and then say, "But that's okay." After about three repetitions of that phrase, I interrupted him. I turned to the congregation and said, "Friends, can we just agree that this is *not* okay!? Oppression is alive and well in Jamestown, New York!" We entered into a time of prayer for him and one of our women, gifted in prophecy, came forward. She broke through the small crowd of people gathered around our brother and knelt before him. She reached up and grabbed his hands and began to weep. She said, "I feel I need to come before you on behalf of the generational white church and ask you for forgiveness. Will you forgive us?" With deep emotion, our brother answered, "Yes." There is a blessed peace that comes in the wake of repentance and forgiveness.

To be led by the presence of God does not indicate that we cease to plan or prepare. It is about margins. The two instances I listed above are two out of the many Sundays we have worshiped together. There have been, however, many Sundays where what is planned is what is done, and the Holy Spirit moves mightily in our midst. Alongside the planning and doing, however, there must be margins in both time and expectation. We must hold our plans with open hands, not clenched fists, understanding that God, at His sole discretion, may change them at any moment.

To be led by the presence of God means we spend much time in prayer. How can we expect to be led by One with whom we have no communion? To say that prayer is weak in our churches today is a gross understatement. Perhaps your church is different, but in our church, social events still get a better attendance than prayer meetings.

In January 2011, the same morning that God released me from preaching that sermon on divorce, I concluded my message on prayer with a challenge. I said, "Next Sunday I am going to be here at 8:00 a.m. for an hour of prayer before anything else is done. Our church is going to be a praying church. I invite you to join me." I recall more than a handful of amens from the congregation. When the following Sunday arrived I entered the empty Sanctuary at 7:30 a.m., determined myself to pray before anyone else arrived. In that moment God spoke to me and said, "How many years are you willing to do this alone if no one else comes?" I had to determine that prayer would be my priority even if it was not for anyone else. Thankfully, God has brought others to pray, and our Wednesday night prayer meetings and Sunday morning hour of prayer are rich and full of the power and presence of the Holy Spirit.

To be led by the presence of God means pastors must trust the leading of God in others. Pastors who insist on controlling their congregations are adhering to the false assumption that God only speaks to and through Pastors. How did we arrive at the clergy/laity model of church when the only scriptural precedent is the image of an interdependent body? Some of the most spiritually rich times in our church have come when God has led us, His church, through His words given to *others* in our body, not just from me.

I was once approached by three different members of our church. One had a vision and the other two felt God had a specific message for our body that was given to them. I gathered together nine spiritually sound and gifted people with wisdom and discernment for a meeting to discuss what God was saying. My personal role in the meeting was to help us synthesize the pieces into a cohesive whole. First the vision was spoken. It would confront us with the thought that if we as a church body would be destroyed, it would be from within and we needed to heed a warning to cease all unkindness, gossip, and ill-speaking between members of our body. Second, the Word was shared regarding a warning to our body against idolatry. Finally, the last message was discussed regarding the valley of dry bones. The point was that God could make us into a mighty army if we would be put together by the hand of God and filled with His Spirit. It was decided by mutual consensus that three messages would be delivered from the pulpit. The first would be our sister, Faith, addressing the issue of idolatry. The second would be preached by myself and another of our young leaders, Heidi, addressing the vision of ill-speaking lurking in our body. Lastly, our brother John would deliver the message concerning the valley of dry bones. The Holy Spirit used the body to speak to the needs of the body, discern their meaning, and preach their message. In order for that to happen, I needed to relinquish all control to the Holy Spirit. I did… it was glorious!

By the way, here is some proof… a copy of the white board from our session:

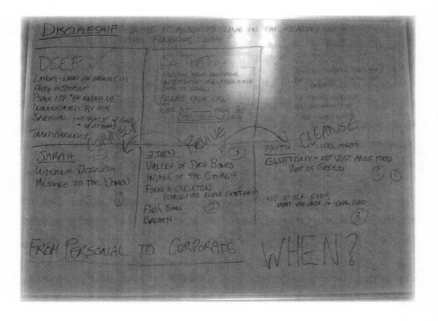

The Power and Presence is unsearchable.

Ask for the ancient path of unending searching.

> "Call to me and I will answer you and tell you
> great and unsearchable things you do not know."
> (Jeremiah 33:3)

Those among us who hunger and thirst after the power and presence of the Holy Spirit have seen a glimpse of the unsearchable riches of God. One glimpse creates an insatiable hunger for more. More of God, more love to share, more of His power, more boldness to search out the lost and show them the way home... more! I, too, have captured the hunger and have met many who share in its resulting drive and desire to go after all God would give.

Would I dare to stand before my Lord one great and glorious day and think I could muster words that would excuse my apathy should I stop searching? Yes, God is gracious and merciful to sinners and the weak, but if my eyes have been opened, if my heart has been captivated, if I have tasted and seen that the Lord is good, there must only be forward movement in Him. Stagnation, for me, would be far worse than death.

The church is spiritual. The church's distinctive attribute, out of all humanity, is the power and presence of the Holy Spirit. How will you address the hunger that is already lurking in the hearts of people within our churches? Will you set them free? Will you accept the call to run the race on the ancient path of God's unsearchable riches? Will we open avenues in our rigid constructs to allow the Holy Spirit to move in the way of His choosing? Will we relinquish all control? Do you leave margins in your plans, allowing for His voice and leading?

Stand, look, ask for the ancient paths ... then *decide.*

CHAPTER FOUR

Prayer, Heart, Fasting and Authority

At the Crossroads of Heaven and Earth

Four ways heaven touches earth and earth touches heaven.

Holiness, which is inseparably connected to the power and presence of the Holy Spirit, creates a natural segue to the next topic of exploration. Prayer is admittedly something all Christians have partaken in at one point or another in their lives. Ask any Christian if they pray and they will answer, "Yes." Even for those questioning their belief in God, they will occasionally reach out to heaven with a prayer saying, "God, if you're out there…".

However, bring up fasting; a heart that breaks for sin, the poor, the broken, and the lost; or ask when the last time was that they used the authority provided in the name of Jesus to heal or cast out a demon; and affirmative responses dwindle to near nothingness.

Prayer, heart, fasting, and authority have untapped potential in the life of a disciple of Jesus. I truly believe that if a poll was taken of most of our church members, the vast majority of them would respond (if honest) to the following questions in the following ways:

+ Describe your prayer life: "I pray, but not as often as I should."
+ How has God broken your heart for others? "I have some unsaved loved ones and that bothers me."
+ How often do you fast? "You know, I can't because I have a medical condition. Honestly, I've never understood it. I give up Facebook for Lent. That's fasting, right?"
+ How has God used you, with His authoritative name, to heal or to command an evil spirit to "go"? "What? … no."

Prayer, heart-engagement, fasting and authority. These are four ways that the Kingdom of God is established on earth. In all four, heaven touches earth and earth touches heaven. Carnality and worldliness, however, have insidiously crept into all four and thereby have handcuffed believers from the power available to them. Our prayer is carnal, many times selfish, many times aimed at worldly things; our hearts break only for ourselves and those things closest to us. We take a break from using the television or cell phone and call that "fasting" to our shame and error. We have no idea what immense power God has given us in the Holy, Mighty, and Authoritative name of Jesus, nor do we disciple people to use that authority.

At the crossroads of heaven and earth, God desires to teach us, disciple us, awaken us to our carnal condition, and empower us to serve Him in ways that establish His Kingdom on earth. It's time to stand at those crossroads and look at our own weak condition. We must then ask for the ancient path of holiness power and rise into our true calling. So let's examine not four individual disciplines, but a singular, yet four-fold discipline of power that God has given us to see mountains moved and be thrown into the sea.

Prayer

It was the morning that marked one week… one week since beginning my retreat away with God at the camp. On that morning, God called me back to the abandoned railroad tracks. The week had been full of glorious moments, honest moments, quiet moments, moments where God was speaking clearly, and moments where it seemed He intentionally withheld His voice. Today, God wanted to speak to me again at the old path.

As I looked over the tracks, I felt impressed to go get my camera. I believed God was asking me to capture a memory. The weather at camp that week had gone from sunny and warm to rainy and cold. This particular morning, peeks of warm sunshine were glimmering through the trees. It was a crisp, unseasonably cold morning following a midnight rain; highly peculiar for mid-August, even in Western

New York. Before leaving to get my camera I left my journal and Bible at the site and told God they were my "token and pledge" that I would return. On the walk back to my cabin, the sun hid itself behind dark gray clouds and I sighed, thinking I had lost my opportunity for a picture of the old path that included the beautiful, early morning sun.

I retrieved my camera and walked back up the hill. As I crested the top of the ravine where the old tracks were, I heard rustling. When I looked up, three deer were there. They were startled by my presence but only wandered a short distance, then stopped and turned back in my direction. They stood still and simply watched. Just then, the sun reappeared from behind the clouds. I smiled as I photographed the site. Like a flood, God began to speak.

> "Those who live near the path of holiness embody the words of the Psalmist who said, 'As the deer pants for streams of water, so my soul pants for you, O God. My soul thirsts for God, for the living God. When can I go and meet with God?' (Psalms 42:1-2) Thirsty souls pray, and those who walk the path of holiness have thirsty souls."

Thirsty souls pray. Indeed. The Living Water that will satisfy our souls is found in the Source of the Living Water and we access that very Source in prayer. God had reminded me that wherever true holiness is found, prayer is right there as its inseparable companion. Wherever soul-thirst is found, prayer is found.

Prayer touches heaven.

Prayer is the avenue by which we touch heaven. It is impossible for a person to claim to be in Christ and not pray. Prayer is the natural result of a holy life and a holy life is the natural result of prayer. To be a Christian immediately demands relationship with God through faith in Jesus Christ, and the natural result of that relationship is prayer. Prayer brings us into close communion with God, gives us release from our burdens and cares, strengthens our faith, and is the entrance into the very throne room of heaven. This should make us cry out with the Psalmist, "When can I go and meet with God?" (Psalms 42:2) We can go at any time. He is ready to engage with us as we pray. Jesus prayed. He prayed much and He prayed often. He prayed early in the morning, in solitude, in public, and on the cross. His disciples, asked to be taught to pray, and Jesus taught them, and us, by beginning with the words, "When you pray…". In Christianity, prayer is implied. However, carnality has crept into our praying and our worldliness must be dealt with if we would have the soul-thirst that drives true prayer.

Carnality is the enemy of prayer.

Prayer has an enemy. It is this world and the nagging, day-to-day activities that call us away from the feet of Jesus and into both the necessary and optional details of our carnal lives. If we would go into the throne room of heaven, carnality will be there, both grabbing us from behind to keep us from moving toward the door and planted in the doorway to keep us from entering.

> "Watch and pray so that you will not fall into temptation. The spirit is willing, but the body is weak." (Matthew 26:41)

> "No, I beat my body and make it my slave..." (1 Corinthians 9:27a)

No one is exempt from the carnal struggles that stand in opposition to prayer. We seek heaven in prayer and earth barks out at us to return to its demands. The more diligently we seek heaven, the louder the earthly barks become. This is frustrating to any child of God and so, for many, the return to the carnal is just flat-out easier than beating our bodies and making them our slaves. We know we should pray – our minds, hearts and reasoning know it to be true - but we end up neglecting prayer and give that time to the world's demands.

The world's demands draw us to intend to pray without actually praying. Haven't we all told people we will pray for their request, but that is really code for, "You have my well wishes, but I really won't pray." Spoken intentions to pray that are not backed up with actual praying are very deceptive to both others and ourselves.

When God called me away to the retreat at the camp, I had no idea how loud the world would bark. At the outset I was so very determined to maintain what I intended: ten days, alone with God, intent on listening to Him, with no interruptions. It didn't take long for that vision to begin to shake, crack and crumble. I knew of two obligations in the middle of the retreat, but decided to keep them due to the fact that they had been on the calendar for a while and I thought it wise not to cancel them. Of course I wanted to be in the pulpit at my church on the Sunday that landed in the midst of the retreat, so that remained on the calendar. The second day of the retreat was a medical appointment for myself for which I had waited a few weeks. Another night was a dinner appointment with two parishioners that my wife and I preferred not to cancel. I also had a loved one who was ill and there were others who wanted to schedule appointments with me and insisted, with great urgency, that they be answered.

Although it seems like I was not winning the war to be on retreat, stay in prayer and remain on-task, I can assure you I have never fought a tougher battle with the enemy than I did over that retreat. I would not give up, give in, or turn away from God's call. I kept what few commitments I had made, and then immediately returned to the camp over and over again. I drove back-and-forth, or returned there late at night if need be to be alone with God. I directly related to Paul in the beating of my body. I had to make it my slave. I *did* turn off the phone more than any other time in my life. I *did* ignore many of the barking sounds and turned my ears to God. I *did* fight and I *did* win many of the battles.

And God honored the fight. He spoke. Like never before in my life. I refused to give up the fight and God refused to give up on me. I did not fulfill the vision conjured up in my own mind that would have made the retreat perfect. But God manifested Himself in my commitment to Him and took my imperfect retreat and used it for His purposes. My soul-thirst for time with God, not compulsion to obey or fulfill an obligation, drove me to fight the good fight.

Apathy in prayer is giving up the fight.

I trust you can see that I, like you, struggle with prayer. The people in my church pray more than ever and yet the fight against carnality is right there all the time. I personally hunger for more and more prayer in my personal life, but the world pushes back. Schedules and commitments call to me. My wife and I desire to pray more together, and yet there are a thousand excuses breathing their false justification for neglecting prayer and trying to lure us away. But our soul-thirst must prevail and we must pray. Leaving the battlefield defeated is simply unthinkable.

To regularly neglect prayer, to the place where we feel we can easily "do church" without it, is to be deceived and hypnotized by the devil himself. Apathy toward prayer is sin – plain and clear. Rest assured, everyone who attends worship on Sundays bows their head as their pastor or other leader prays. We may occasionally pray a short blessing over our meals, and we certainly pray for emergency needs when they surprise us. However, rich, unhurried, conversational, emotional, joyful, heart-wrenching, deep, weeping, celebrating, groaning, meaningful prayer has escaped us. It does not matter to what degree it has escaped us, and perhaps your prayer life is highly fulfilling and meaningful at this moment. Should that stop us from searching out the unsearchable riches of God in prayer? Even if your personal prayer life seems rich and at full capacity, there is more of God to be known and found. There are greater depths and heights. No one would disagree with the benefits of more prayer, regardless of your current place in your spiritual life.

Holiness overcomes the neglect of prayer

To overcome apathy toward prayer doesn't require any formulas or forms. You won't need a specific book of pre-written prayers. You won't even need a list of things to pray for. All of those may be good and useful tools, but they will never snap us out of the apathetic, hypnotic trance that numbs our desire for prayer. The apathy must be dealt with first or all our other efforts will be futile. The war will be won if we continually launch a rebellion against carnality, deal with our soul, and become highly thirsty for the things of God.

> Whom have I in heaven but you? And earth has
> nothing I desire besides you. My flesh and my heart

may fail, but God is the strength of my heart and my portion forever. (Psalms 73:25-26)

O God, you are my God, earnestly I seek you; my soul thirsts for you, my body longs for you, in a dry and weary land where there is no water. (Psalms 63:1)

Better is one day in your courts than a thousand elsewhere; I would rather be a doorkeeper in the house of my God than dwell in the tents of the wicked. (Psalms 84:10)

The war against carnality is won when we love the world less and love God more. With great assurance I can tell you that if you want to become a person with a deep, full life of prayer in rich relationship with God, unlike anything you thought possible, begin by falling more in love with God. When your heart fully resonates with the psalmist's words, "earnestly I seek You" … "earth has nothing I desire besides You" … "Better is one day in Your courts…" the consecration of your devotion to God will draw you into prayer like an irresistible magnet. Whatever you love most, you will feed the most.

Prayer is reciprocal love

Out of God's love, He reaches out to us with an invitation to touch heaven in prayer. Through our love for Him, our thirsty souls accept the invitation. God is pleased to answer and heaven touches earth. Love meets love, heaven and earth unite. This is God's beautiful design of prayer for those with thirsty souls. Love is the only motivator suitable for prayer. God will not guilt us into praying, nor will He compel us to pray. Our love for Him, reaching out with a thirsty soul, recognizing His love for us, is the most excellent way of prayer. This love will break through the apathy that keeps us from praying.

Heart

> Jesus wept. (John 11:35)

We love God ...we pray. Out of that we may come to realize that God has additional plans for our hearts that will reflect the death-to-self of holiness. Our hearts must love like God's and break like God's for the broken condition of the world. Love that is imprisoned in our hearts is not love at all. Love becomes true love when it is directed and expressed toward others. When Jesus wept, His heart was broken not just because His friend Lazarus had died, but over the grief of those who were hurting and over the death-condition of lost humanity. Jesus knew He came to do something about death but He also could see firsthand that the curse of death was still upon the world.

In Jesus, human tears flowed from heaven's eyes.

Have you truly asked God to give you the same heart as Jesus? The core message of holiness is contained in this: the singular purpose of our lives to join Christ in His work, the heart that responds to earth's brokenness like Christ's, and the perfecting of our love to be like His. Does your heart respond to the world's brokenness with Christ-like weeping? Why have we removed holy heartbreak from our message? Must we be entertained in our churches to the point where any shred of discomfort is not allowed? Jesus was holy, and His life centered on His singular holy mission. He calls all of us to join Him in that mission. Have your human eyes ever cried heaven's tears because you saw what heaven sees?

> Blessed are you who hunger now, for you will be satisfied. Blessed are you who weep now, for you will laugh. (Luke 6:21)

Holiness overcomes apathy of heart.

"Because of the increase of wickedness, the love of
most will grow cold,…" (Matthew 24:12)

"And now these three remain: faith, hope and love.
But the greatest of these is love." (1 Corinthians 13:13)

In his dissertation, "A Plain Account of Christian Perfection,"
John Wesley described holiness as the "perfecting of love." Even
though we still maintain our humanity and therefore may act in
ignorance, make mistakes, be infirmed in many ways, or manifest "a
thousand nameless defects" in our flesh, we *can* be perfected in our
love for God and our fellow man. The reason "the greatest of these is
love," is that love is the only thing that will follow us into heaven. In
love's absence, our hate and apathy will befriend us in hell.

We simply must not, and cannot, allow our love to grow cold
in spite of the brokenness around us. Our hearts must be engaged.
Prayer is birthed from a fully engaged heart. We pray for the things
that break our hearts. Many find it difficult to pray for nameless
people in photos from around the world even though the pictures
display horrific poverty, malnutrition, genocide, war and disease.
Why? Our hearts haven't broken for them. If we're honest, it's just
easier to turn a blind eye to the world's troubles and ignore them. We
ignore the problems and disengage from the people going through
them.

We are people who experience emotions. God knit them into
our being. Why do we seek to squash emotions in worship? Do we
so fear the very hint of fanaticism that we deny the experience of
emotion in worship? I see Jesus as a man of great passion. He wept
and overturned tables in the Temple. He agonized before the Father
in the Garden of Gethsemane and told the Pharisees that their father
was the devil. He pronounced blessings and woes. Our worship and
our lives must be passionate and emotional. If you find it difficult to

think in terms of worship and service to God as emotional, ask God to warm your cold heart.

Launching a rebellion for a tender heart.

If we fear our love has grown cold, simply sitting idle and expecting a change to magically happen will not melt the ice around our hearts. We must take notice of our pitiful condition, become disgusted with our own apathy and coldness of heart, and launch an inner rebellion for the sake of love.

> "But love your enemies, do good to them, and lend to them without expecting to get anything back. Then your reward will be great, and you will be sons of the Most High, because he is kind to the ungrateful and wicked." (Luke 6:35)

The simplest way to launch the rebellion? Heed the command of Jesus to engage with your enemies in love. Jesus' words are not suggestions. They insist we take action. To love your enemies means that you have actively chosen to love them. This is the way God loves. He chooses to love those who do not love Him. He reaches out to those who turn their backs toward Him. He died for those who wanted to see Him dead. God loves. God is love. God commands us to love. While I was still a sinner, God loved me, and while you were a still a sinner, God loved you (paraphrase of Romans 5:8).

Where our hearts are tender, we will pray. Where our hearts break, we will intercede. Tenderness and brokenness of heart is the holy way to which God calls us. Broken hearts touch heaven and heaven touches broken hearts.

Fasting

Fasting: Another way heaven touches earth.

> "When you fast, do not look somber as the hypocrites do, for they disfigure their faces to show men they are fasting. I tell you the truth, they have received their reward in full. (Matthew 6:16)

> Jesus answered, "How can the guests of the bridegroom fast while he is with them? They cannot, so long as they have him with them. But the time will come when the bridegroom will be taken from them, and on that day they will fast. (Mark 2:19-20)

> Then Jesus was led by the Spirit into the desert to be tempted by the devil. After fasting forty days and forty nights, he was hungry. (Matthew 4:1-2)

In his book, *Fasting: the Ancient Practices*, author Scot McKnight says, "Fasting is the natural, inevitable response of a person to a grievous sacred moment in life."[2]

Our human flesh, that God made and called "very good", has been mostly removed from our worship, sermons, teaching, exhortations and spiritual discussions. However, our bodies should naturally join the mind and soul/spirit, being an equal partner in our spiritual experiences. One of the ways heaven touches earth and earth touches heaven is when spiritual disruptions become physical disruptions. We are complete beings: mind, soul/spirit and body. The body must be welcomed back into the church's ongoing teaching and conversation concerning holiness and make fasting should be part of the conversation and practice for holiness people. This is the main

---

[2]   McKnight, Scot (2009-02-10). Fasting: The Ancient Practices . Thomas Nelson.

premise of Scot McKnight's book which I would wholeheartedly recommend as good reading for understanding on this topic.

McKnight's definition has shed new light into my understanding in regards to fasting. "Grievous, sacred moments" revealed to me an understanding of closeness to God where my heart and His would beat as one and His view of things would become mine. The ways God grieves sin would merge with my own life and the ways He grieves the result of sin would become my ways too. However, it was equally amazing to me that McKnight suggests my body and yours would respond to these moments with fasting. In fact, his use of the words "natural" and "inevitable" to describe the body's impulse to fast make perfect sense to me as they are applied to the Biblical text.

Fasting mirrors the contents of the heart.

If God would answer us affirmatively as we pray for a broken heart that matches that of Jesus who wept over Jerusalem, then we would understand fasting and we would actually fast. When we fast, the condition of our heart is reflected in our actions. Fasting is not designed to get God to do something for me. Fasting is a reflection of what God is doing in me. Fasting is one way human flesh responds to the touch of heaven. When we fast, we tangibly express that something heavenly has happened in our hearts that can't be said or sung with words. The story of Anna, found in Luke's gospel, tells of how a grievous, sacred moment drove her to a life of prayer and fasting.

> There was also a prophetess, Anna, the daughter of Phanuel, of the tribe of Asher. She was very old; she had lived with her husband seven years after her marriage, and then was a widow until she was eighty-four. She never left the temple but worshiped night and day, fasting and praying. (Luke 2:36-37)

Anna's "holy grief" over the loss of her husband manifested itself in a life of prayer and fasting. In the end, God allowed her eyes to behold Jesus. Jesus suggested that His disciples would fast as a result of mourning after his departure from this world. The denial of self in regards to food, therefore indicates that a far more important work is going on in the heart. As the spiritual need rises above and takes precedent over the natural need, we will first give our attention to the spiritual need. Food can wait.

Fasting begets focus.

To fast is to give our full attention to God. We remove food from our lives and upset the daily rhythm to which we are accustomed. In the "upset," we go before God. We pray. Our hearts may be captivated by a holy moment of grief or concern. We open ourselves up completely to God and let Him in. We do not announce our fast to the world. We simply move from moment-to-moment, allowing the Holy Spirit to captivate our minds and draw us into prayer. In the cessation of food we learn the rhythm of "praying without ceasing." (1 Thessalonians 5:17)

In the rhythm of prayer we are fully focused on God, and our spiritual senses are heightened and awakened. In the second chapter I told you my personal story of death to self. What I have learned in each significant moment of surrender to God is that the Holy Spirit first reveals to me what is yet to be surrendered. Then, He gently, firmly, and truthfully begins to draw me to the place of surrender. When I have fasted, the areas of my life in need of surrender come into clear focus. Having surrendered food to give my entire mind and heart to God, I am perfectly postured to surrender even more to Christ. This kind of surrender requires focus and fasting provides the focus.

My retreat at the camp was for the purpose of focus. For the Christian, fasting is a walking retreat... a blessed retreat in the everyday rhythm of life with intense focus on God, His desires, and His heart.

Fasting begets self-control.

Fasting is holy. Gluttony is unholy. Food is necessary for life and health. Excessive amounts of food actually deteriorates health. Daniel gave up certain foods as a sign of his devotion to God and God's holy law. Could it be suggested that most churches don't teach fasting or encourage the practice of fasting; that we don't warn against gluttony or intrude on the personal issue of the results of gluttony; that we don't call our people to holy fasts because of our overall apathy towards holiness? Holiness indicates the power and presence of the Holy Spirit, which gives birth to the fruit of the Spirit in the human life. Self-control is part of the equation but should not be equated with *will power*. Will power is a person's attempt to gain control over the body by exercising intense will of the mind. That is not how God works. As we give up our will in exchange for God's will, His Spirit and His will come and invade our minds and give us "the mind of Christ." (1 Corinthians 2:16) With our will dead and God's will alive in us, self-control is under God's control. Those who live in self-control through the power of the Spirit will fast.

Fasting reminds us that, "Man cannot live on bread alone."

> But you are a shield around me, O LORD; you bestow glory on me and lift up my head. To the LORD I cry aloud, and he answers me from his holy hill. Selah. I lie down and sleep; I wake again, because the LORD sustains me. (Psalms 3:3-5)

Who sustains your life? Is it not the LORD? When we fast we can either *rest*, knowing we are sustained by His great power, or we can *wrest*, worrying about our hunger and our health. I know that many will seek to dispute this claim or suggest that I should include some sort of medical disclaimer for those who should not go without food or follow doctor's orders. Allow me to speak, then, out of my own experience and point us all in the direction of our God who formed all of us from the dust. His breath within us is our breath of life. He can, at His sole discretion, take my life at this very moment or allow it to continue. Jesus restored sight to the blind, and I believe He can sustain me while I fast. When I have fasted, I have never suffered any ill effects but the illness in my soul subsided greatly. Fasting has never caused me physical illness, and has cured spiritual illness. What glory!

Will you taste and see that the Lord is good in the beauty of fasting? Will you launch an inner rebellion against all apathy or disdain for fasting? To ask for the ancient path of fasting requires that you confront self and put it to death. For the greater church, we must recognize our general lack of this discipline, encourage it, and teach it to our people. Why? Because Jesus fasted; because Jesus taught fasting to His disciples; because fasting changes us; because fasting reflects the contents of the human heart; because fasting strengthens our spirit though the flesh may be weak; because fasting is holy.

Authority

Imagine driving down the highway one day and you look in your rear-view mirror. Your see a black-and-white automobile with red, blue, and white flashing lights right on your bumper. Immediately you begin to questions yourself. "What did I do? Was I driving too fast?" You pull over to the side of the road. No other car or truck you encounter on the highway will cause you to experience this panic and dread; no other vehicle will cause you to pull over to the side of the road. So what is it about a *police car* that makes you pull over? *Authority.*

You know how this works. The police officer in the car behind you has the authority to enforce the laws of the highway. If you have been a law-breaker, you will be called to account, and should you choose to resist their authority, things will only get worse. If you are a good, law abiding citizen, you understand the nature of the officer's authority, and you fully submit to the officer's demands.

Authority in the spirit realm.

> Then Jesus came to them and said, "All authority in heaven and on earth has been given to me." (Matthew 28:18)

> "And these signs will accompany those who believe: In my name they will drive out demons; they will speak in new tongues; they will pick up snakes with their hands; and when they drink deadly poison, it will not hurt them at all; they will place their hands on sick people, and they will get well." After the Lord Jesus had spoken to them, he was taken up into heaven and he sat at the right hand of God. Then the disciples went out and preached everywhere, and the Lord worked with them and confirmed his word by the signs that accompanied it. (Mark 16:17-20)

From the previous chapter, you will remember these things we affirmed about the spiritual nature of the Church:

- We serve a God who is Spirit.
- His Kingdom is spiritual.
- His gifts are spiritual.
- His enemies are spiritual.
- The weapons with which we fight the enemy are spiritual.
- The power we are given is spiritual.
- Our prayer must be spiritual.
- Our expectations must be for the supernatural.

God's supernatural power is not only manifested through spiritual gifts. His power is also manifested each time we speak His name with authority to push back the darkness. There is supernatural power in speaking the name of Jesus. The authority needed for doing God's Kingdom-establishing, enemy-overcoming work in this world can only be given to us by Christ Jesus, who has been given all authority by His Father. Jesus' authority is all powerful: at the sound of His name, the enemy must leave. Pleading the blood of Jesus causes demons to shriek. Remember, the demons believe in God... and shudder! This is all because of the authority given us in the name of Jesus.

> He called his twelve disciples to him and gave them authority to drive out evil spirits and to heal every disease and sickness. (Matthew 10:1)

Following Jesus' ascension into heaven, the scriptures record that the disciples of Jesus did the very things Jesus asked, using the very authority Jesus gave them.

> Then Peter said, "Silver or gold I do not have, but what I have I give you. In the name of Jesus Christ of Nazareth, walk." Taking him by the right hand, he helped him up, and instantly the man's feet and ankles became strong. He jumped to his feet and began to walk. Then he went with them into the temple courts, walking and jumping, and praising God. (Acts 3:6-8)

Heaven touches earth through Christ's authority.

When humans (though we have no spiritual authority of our own) take the authority given to us by our King and command demons to go, command flesh to be healed, command cripples to walk, or command the dead to be raised, heaven descends to earth and the supernatural blasts through the natural. While prayer is conversation with and petition to God, using the authority we've been given means we can, at Christ's directive, command things to happen in the Name of Jesus. What a marvelous gift! Why do we see so little uses of God's authoritative power and might being displayed through His children? Where holiness lacks, there are few demonstrations of the Spirit's power through the authority of Jesus' name. Where holiness abounds, captives are set free!

Apathy towards authority.

Today it seems that churches are delighted about expanding their facilities and organizational structures. These worldly things, with all of the management and time-consuming, money-consuming activity they demand of us, do not directly do the work of expanding the Kingdom of God on earth. Building expansion requires a general contractor. Building the Kingdom of God requires holy people of God who are known in the heavenly realms because of their prayer, their heart, their love and their devotion to the King. The power and authority to drive out the enemy of God's Kingdom is freely given to holy people.

We attend church services and church social events. However, where is the power? Church, we must launch a rebellion against our apathy to the mighty power of God. We must seek God to be granted this authority so that these words will be made manifest on our world:

> "The kingdom of the world has become the kingdom of our Lord and of his Christ, and he will reign for ever and ever." (Revelation 11:15)

The convergence of the four-fold power.

It is one thing to pray. It another thing to add a passionate heart for the world's broken condition to our prayer. It is yet another thing to fast out of devotion to, or in response to, our heartbreak. It is still another thing to command demons with the authoritative name of Jesus. Individually, any one of these disciplines is encouraged and good. But imagine the kind of power that would emerge from one person who would embody all four of these holy disciplines! Where heaven regularly touches earth in and through Jesus' disciples through prayer, heart, fasting and authority, there you will see the Kingdom of God come and His will be done on earth as it is in heaven.

One particular account from Matthew's gospel describes perfectly why the disciples' attempt to drive out a demon failed. It likely reflects the very same reasons our ministry attempts have become so carnal and void of God's power and authority.

> When they came to the crowd, a man approached Jesus and knelt before him. "Lord, have mercy on my son," he said. "He has seizures and is suffering greatly. He often falls into the fire or into the water. I brought him to your disciples, but they could not heal him." "O unbelieving and perverse generation," Jesus replied, "how long shall I stay with you? How long shall I put up with you? Bring the boy here to me." Jesus rebuked the demon, and it came out of the boy, and he was healed from that moment. Then the disciples came to Jesus in private and asked, "Why couldn't we drive it out?" He replied, "Because you have so little faith. I tell you the truth, if you have faith as small as a mustard seed, you can say to this mountain, 'Move from here to there' and it will move. Nothing will be impossible for you." But this kind does not go out except by prayer and fasting. (Matthew 17:14-21)

Prayer ... fasting ... faith. Then, and only then, take the authority. And, when we do, nothing will be impossible for us. *Nothing!*

I'm certain that Jesus has not changed His position on Kingdom expansion and establishment. He still wants to use us to expand and establish His Kingdom, if we will shed the apathetic, carnal responses to prayer, fasting and the like, and allow our hearts to be stirred for the timeless behaviors of disciples. Will we be people of prayer or merely pray now and then? Will we allow our hearts to break for the brokenness and lost condition of the world or will we continue to wear blinders on our hearts? Will we, allowing our body to be part of our worship, fast as a reflection of what is in our heart or will we continue to live life on our own terms? Finally, will we seek God in those three disciplines for His authority, to do His work as He calls, or will we continue to be satisfied with organizational church-as-usual?

As we stand at the crossroads of heaven and earth, let us ask for the ancient paths of prayer, heart-break, fasting, and Kingdom authority. Thirsty souls pray, thirsty souls have tender hearts, thirsty souls fast and thirsty souls are granted Kingdom authority. How thirsty is your soul?

CHAPTER FIVE

Repentance

At the Crossroads of Sin and Forgiveness

After ten days of retreat with God, my last evening at the camp had arrived. When I started my time with God nine days earlier, I truly wondered how I would make it so long in complete solitude. However, my final night made me realize how much I would miss these times. I also feared the loss of the special quality of the Spirit's voice upon my departure for home the next afternoon.

For me, camp is not complete without a campfire, so I decided a fire would be a nice way to end my final evening. I acquired some firewood and set out to start my fire. To make the campfire experience complete, I wanted to roast some hot dogs for dinner and enjoy the peace at the fireside. But, as luck would have it, things didn't quite go as planned. I've started campfires before so this was a calculated, familiar exercise. Dozens of times this formula has never let me down. Start with a bed of crinkled up newspaper, add some dry kindling twigs, use your handy butane lighter and you're all set. Once the fire starts you place your dry logs on and "Voila!"... fire!

Nope... not tonight.

This fire just didn't want to start. At one point, it seemed the newspaper was actually resisting combustion. The twigs were dry and snapped easily, but they wouldn't light either. Finally some cotton balls dipped in petroleum jelly seemed to maintain the fire long enough for me to roast *one* hot dog. God began to prod me. "Will you come back into the cottage and write?" All I wanted was a fire. I barely got the second hot dog roasted before all flames went out and billows of smoke rose from the fire pit. I said, "Well Lord, it looks like I'm writing tonight. Yes, I'll go back into the cottage."

I proceeded to put everything away except for my lawn chair. Through the smoke I saw a handful of embers left in the bottom of the fire pit. My last act of surrender was tossing my used paper plate into the pit and then headed in. After tidying up inside I went out for the lawn chair. The fire was in full blaze. Everything was burning! I couldn't help but look up and chuckle.

I sat down in the lawn chair and just shook my head. The fire was burning so hot that I thought I would have to move my chair further away to avoid a potential burn. I let out a sigh. Just then, God spoke:

"When you surrendered to Me, I lit the fire."

I sat for a while pondering God's words and enjoyed a fire that was literally consuming everything that had refused to burn just moments earlier. In the loving way that only God can, He showed me that surrender is the key to every fire God wants to light in the human heart; therefore, where there is no fire, there is no submission. If there is no submission, then repentance is needed.

At the crossroads of sin and forgiveness, we must seek the ancient path of repentance.

> "...if my people, who are called by my name, will humble themselves and pray and seek my face and turn from their wicked ways, then will I hear from heaven and will forgive their sin and will heal their land." (2 Chronicles 7:14)

Repentance isn't just for those at the threshold of accepting Christ through faith. Peter's first sermon on the day of Pentecost was preached to people who were made aware of their sin and told of the amazing salvation available to them through Jesus. Their response to the Gospel message was, "Brothers, what shall we do?" (Acts 2:37) Because they had yet to hear of or believe in Jesus, they were instructed to "repent and be baptized." (Acts 2:38) For everyone who follows Christ, this initial repentance in necessary, but we must realize that there is also a need for repentance beyond the point of salvation. Indeed, repentance is not a once-and-for-all kind of thing. The closer we get to Jesus and the more we seek to surrender all to Him, we should expect to regularly encounter a rhythm of repentance that follows us through life.

Part of the deception of the church is that we believe we couldn't possibly have anything amiss within us for which to repent, yet God, throughout the biblical text, has regularly been in the habit of calling His people to repentance. The gospels are full of accounts where Jesus calls the Jews and even the disciples to repent. In the epistles, Paul and the other Apostles speak correctively to the church, and call them to repent time and time again. In Revelation, John prophetically records Jesus' words to the seven churches in Asia Minor, and nearly all of them receive words of correction and calls to repentance.

Just because we have assurance in our salvation doesn't mean God won't correct us along the way. Just because we call ourselves Christian doesn't mean we won't grieve the Holy Spirit or disobey the leading of God. People seeking to live holy lives love God and obey Him out of that love. When we fail to obey we should be quick to repent.

Fire follows submission.

God showed me through a campfire that He will light a fire in people and churches when they fully surrender to Him. In light of this, allow me to be direct. The fire is missing in our churches, in our ministries, and in our people. The fire represents the power and presence of the Holy Spirit, manifesting Himself in supernatural power that transforms individuals and produces true spiritual fruit. Contrast that image to the predictable, stagnant state of most churches today and you will notice the missing fire. Here is just a sampling of the ways the fire is missing:

+ Fire is missing in churches that are viewed as dispensers of religious goods and services to be shopped by Christian *consumers*. Fire is present in a body of people who are passionate to change the world and serving Christ's Kingdom under His Divine Headship.
+ Fire is missing in our evangelism, that is weak at best. We have become satisfied with zero conversions, zero baptisms, zero passion, and zero growth. Fire is present when the Lord is regularly adding to the number of those serving His Kingdom.
+ Fire is missing when churches rely on inspiring music, captivating orators, and videos, rather than the power and presence of the Holy Spirit.
+ Fire is missing in churches where spiritual gifts have been reduced to everyday displays of human talent, and especially where the supernatural gifts are largely unwelcome. Fire is present where the full manifestation of the Spirit is welcome and present.
+ Fire is missing when the dreams and visions promised by the prophet Joel have been replaced with two, five, and ten year plans that directly resemble that of secular businesses.

- Fire is missing when we use the word *ministry* to describe programs that are presented for peoples' entertainment. Fire is present when we obey Christ's commands to feed the hungry, clothe the naked, visit or heal the sick, and/or wash peoples' feet as servants.

- Fire is missing when we use the word "faith" to describe easy-to-achieve budgets and hefty endowment funds on which we rely to sustain our facilities and programs. This worldly model, transplanted into the church, leaves no room for God to provide. Fire is present when we rely on God for daily bread and He faithfully provides.

- Fire is missing in many ineffective churches whose communities would not even notice their absence if their doors closed. Fire is present when we realize our mission by serving the community around us, tangibly demonstrating the love of God through acts of service, redemption, deliverance, healing and compassion.

- Fire is missing in churches where the phrase "spiritual growth" means that someone has committed to attend their services, participate in some sort of church job, and give a bit of their money. Fire is present where life-change is taking place on a regular basis.

- Fire is missing in churches where prayer is weak in both pastors and congregations and is more self-centered rather than intercessory.

- Fire is missing in churches where more concern is expressed over a change in the bulletin design or paint color than the concern shown for the hell-bound lost souls in their towns and cities. Fire is present in churches where mission trumps preferences every time.

- Fire is missing in church members who will show up for dinners, concerts, and fellowship events, while prayer meetings, revivals, and discipleship opportunities are neglected or non-existent.

- Fire is missing in pastors whenever they view changes in their pastoral appointments through the lens of promotion rather than calling.

- Fire is missing in churches that don't seek complete victory over sin. Many church members speak in terms of their struggles with sin and worldliness but few seek complete victory over sin. To add to the problem, people within churches are beginning to partly reject the full authority of scripture due to worldly actions that contradict biblical instructions.

- Fire is missing in "preference-based" worship services where people insist on their personal desired tastes in music, modes, methods, and formats to which they have become accustomed. If any of their personal preferences come up missing or are changed in any way, they disengage from worship and complain. Fire is present in children of God who can worship anywhere and in any style.

- Fire is missing in people who want to be known as Christian but also want to keep old worldly habits, behaviors, passions, and priorities. In other words, they simply aren't motivated to surrender all to the Lordship of Christ.

The list goes on. We must wake up to the fact that we have much to repent of. Remember back to the thought presented in the first chapter: Sin can manifest itself not only in the bad things we do, but also in the good things we neglect. In the numbness and apathy within our churches, mountains of good are regularly neglected and sin is allowed to continue unchecked. When these conditions are present, repentance is needed.

> "Then he will say to those on his left, 'Depart from me, you who are cursed, into the eternal fire prepared for the devil and his angels. For I was hungry and you gave me nothing to eat, I was thirsty

and you gave me nothing to drink, I was a stranger and you did not invite me in, I needed clothes and you did not clothe me, I was sick and in prison and you did not look after me.' They also will answer, 'Lord, when did we see you hungry or thirsty or a stranger or needing clothes or sick or in prison, and did not help you?' He will reply, 'I tell you the truth, whatever you did not do for one of the least of these, you did not do for me.' Then they will go away to eternal punishment, but the righteous to eternal life." (Matthew 25:41-46)

Jesus said to them, "Whatever you did not do...". We must pay careful attention to all that our Lord has commanded that we do not do.

The holy way of apology.

Occasionally I have the opportunity to teach pastors, and I've also been mentoring some ministerial candidates in our congregation. One of the questions I like to ask Pastors and leaders is: "When is the last time you said 'I'm sorry' and apologized for something you did wrong?" Apology and a contrite heart is the first part of repentance. Apology is a sign of strength for leaders, not weakness, and not failure. Apology is important because it's not enough to *know* the wrong we do, we must know how to deal with it.

The way of apology is necessary for all Christians. Leaders must model it, but members of the body of Christ must stand ready to apologize at all times. To humble oneself before a sister or brother in holy apology is a beautiful thing. The presence of the ability to apologize indicates a softness of the heart that can only come from the Holy Spirit. In contrast, when members of the body withhold apology, then pride is present and working to destroy relationships through unresolved conflict.

Perform a thorough self-examination. When is the last time you apologized for anything in your church, home, school or place of business? Whom have you forgiven even though they have withheld their apology from you? Are you free of bitterness and resentment? Jesus takes seriously this business of forgiveness. "Forgive us our debts, as we also have forgiven our debtors." (Matthew 6:12) Apologize. Apologize each and every time your behavior or mistakes have made it necessary. Release your life of the bitterness and strife that is caused through demanding justice. Walk the ancient path of repentance by the holy way of apology.

God corrects and disciplines.

One of the many facets of God's character is that He is parental. He is our Father. Therefore, it naturally follows that we, His children, can and should expect to be corrected by our Father. The writer of Hebrews beautifully illustrates the parental nature of our Father and the disciplinary life we should expect as His children.

> And you have forgotten that word of encouragement that addresses you as sons: "My son, do not make light of the Lord's discipline, and do not lose heart when he rebukes you, because the Lord disciplines those he loves, and he punishes everyone he accepts as a son." Endure hardship as discipline; God is treating you as sons. For what son is not disciplined by his father? If you are not disciplined (and everyone undergoes discipline), then you are illegitimate children and not true sons. Moreover, we have all had human fathers who disciplined us and we respected them for it. How much more should we submit to the Father of our spirits and live! Our fathers disciplined us for a little while as they thought best; but God

disciplines us for our good, that we may share in his
holiness. No discipline seems pleasant at the time,
but painful. Later on, however, it produces a harvest
of righteousness and peace for those who have been
trained by it. (Hebrews 12:5-11)

Today, there is a systemic problem in our churches brought about
by a lack of discipline. Because of its uncomfortable feel, we ignore
the ongoing sin problem in peoples' lives to the churches detriment.
With the decline of disciplinary action in our society and the rise
of relativism, the church seems to be adopting these worldly models
instead of God's model of loving correction. If our understanding of
God is that He is merely benevolent, we will have a serious disconnect
in our understanding of both personal and church discipline.

We must repent of relativism in the church. We must shun the
notion that everyone has their own brand of the truth and we are all
okay. We must teach and disciple people to know and understand
God as the kind of Father that loves us so much that He will indeed
discipline us. Holiness blossoms where God's children expect and
submit to discipline. It's time to walk the ancient path of repentance
by the holy way of discipline.

The process of discipline.

God's discipline begins when His people wander from what is
known to be right and into disobedience. The purpose of God's
discipline is to draw us back into the center of His will. God *will* draw
us back into submission to Him if we are resistant. He loves us too
much to leave us in our own disobedience. However, His preference
is to have obedient children who love Him by simply obeying His
commands.

Preemptive instruction (command and obedience).

> "If you love me, you will obey what I command."
> (John 14:15)

Jesus commands. We are to submit to His commands and obey. This is a very simple concept that has been God's way since creation. There were two trees in the center of the Garden of Eden. The command was to eat from one and not from the other. These were simple instructions that somehow were too difficult to follow. The good news about submitting to God is that His commands give us life. His intentions are never to harm, and He will never lead us down wrong paths. When God's people don't follow God's ways, His first step is to intervene with a prophetic voice of intervention.

Voice of intervention (prophetic warning and call to submission).

> …He sent them a prophet, who said, "This is what
> the LORD, the God of Israel, says…" (Judges 6:8a)

If we do not follow the commandments of our Lord, He will lovingly send us warnings. The prophets of old were sent to tell Israel the ways they had disobeyed. God is "slow to anger" and "abounding in love." (Psalm 103:8b) For these reasons, His children are always warned prior to judgment. At the point of warning, humble repentance is the desired response. Not only did Israel ignore many of the prophets, they killed them as well. If God's corrective, prophetic voice were to come our way, would we listen? There is no doubt that God is raising a prophetic voice to His people in our time to abandon the harmful paths of religion and pride and walk the ancient path of holiness. Will we repent, or will we ignore God's voice? Will we recognize the prophetic voice as the voice of God, or will we kill the prophets and seek the voices our itching ears long to hear?

Act of intervention (judgment and corrective action).

> "I will pronounce my judgments on my people because of their wickedness in forsaking me, in burning incense to other gods and in worshiping what their hands have made." (Jeremiah 1:16)

When we refuse to listen to the warning call of God, judgment is imminent. God does not delight in the corrective action of flood and fire, or exile and expulsion. He prefers a contrite heart and humble repentance. If we refuse repentance, God will ultimately act. God's desire is that you and I sacrifice our own will and return to Him with our whole hearts. If we do, there is no intervention necessary and we will be at peace with God, ourselves and others.

Pride and passivity... the enemies of repentance.

> ... All of you, clothe yourselves with humility toward one another, because, "God opposes the proud but gives grace to the humble." (1 Peter 5:5b)

Pride stands in direct opposition to God and God stands in direct opposition to pride. There is absolutely no room for pride in the body of Christ, but those who choose to walk in pride do so to their own detriment, for they will fall headlong into sin. Every moral failure leading to disqualification from service for church leaders begins with pride. God opposes pride by tearing down the thing we take pride in.

> And he told them this parable: "The ground of a certain rich man produced a good crop. He thought to himself, 'What shall I do? I have no place to store my crops.' Then he said, 'This is what I'll do. I will tear down my barns and build bigger ones, and there

I will store all my grain and my goods. And I'll say to myself, "You have plenty of good things laid up for many years. Take life easy; eat, drink and be merry."' But God said to him, 'You fool! This very night your life will be demanded from you. Then who will get what you have prepared for yourself?' This is how it will be with anyone who stores up things for himself but is not rich toward God." (Luke 12:16-21)

Pride is not reserved for individuals. In the church, pride can become part of a congregation's culture or even a denomination's culture. The Jews took pride in the Temple and in their status as God's chosen people. That was not enough to keep them from God's discipline and prophetic reminder that he was watching them.

This is what the LORD Almighty, the God of Israel, says: "Reform your ways and your actions, and I will let you live in this place. Do not trust in deceptive words and say, 'This is the temple of the LORD, the temple of the LORD, the temple of the LORD!'"

'Will you steal and murder, commit adultery and perjury, burn incense to Baal and follow other gods you have not known, and then come and stand before me in this house, which bears my Name, and say, "We are safe"—safe to do all these detestable things? Has this house, which bears my Name, become a den of robbers to you? But I have been watching!" declares the LORD.' (Jeremiah 7:3-4, 9-11)

The Jews lost their focus on the most important things and thought the Temple, their status, and their sacrifices would excuse their idolatry. No, they were not safe. We, too, must not think we are safe just because we have been in a church for years or decades. We are not safe just because we adhere to any particular code of doctrine. We are not safe because of participation in programs. Personal lives of holiness through surrender to Christ, and ridding ourselves and our churches of any and all idols is the only way we can ensure we are safe. Our impact will be measured by our holiness of life and devotion to serving our King in our generation. We will not be safe in the eyes of the Lord unless we are holy, and we can't borrow our grandfather's holy life. We must be obedient.

Is there pride among us? We need to ask for the ancient path of repentance.

I'm not a fan of memorial plaques in churches. To me they represent self-promotion, self-congratulation and self-exaltation. They are just another form of pride. When I first arrived at the church where I currently serve, there were plaques everywhere. Plaques on the piano and organ, plaques in the Fellowship Hall and plaques in the stairwell. Plaques for construction projects and missions trips. There are even names permanently etched in large, old English lettering on each of the three large stained glass windows in the Sanctuary. It took some time, but our church facility is now mostly plaque-free.

Do we want the memorial of our lives to be carved in metal that rusts? Is our contribution to the church merely financial and/or material? Do I want people to remember *me*, thank *me*, and honor *me*? No! May it never be so! I want my life to sing the song of Christ and may I be remembered as one who served the Lord. No other memorial is needed.

Are we memorializing ourselves over Christ? Is pride in us standing in opposition to God? Are there any plaques, trophies, or awards that aid in maintaining our pride? If so, then we need to ask for, and walk humbly on, the ancient path of repentance.

Passivity in people's hearts.

However, beyond the blatant and arrogant nature of pride and its opposition to God and holiness, there is a different kind of offense of which we must repent: passivity. By this I mean the condition where comfort and familiarity in the church has led us to lose our "edge" as Kingdom servants. The motions of church have become so mundane that we rarely feel the Spirit's sting of conviction. We may be comfortable but we are not wholly committed. Church services and programs become our priority at the expense of our actual missional living. We love our churchy things, but our first love suffers.

I had the occasion to preach on repentance at our Family Camp the summer just prior to my retreat there. God had been preparing the message in me for a full year. At the previous year's family camp, the evangelist for the camp, Dr. Tim Dwyer, gave a passionate message from Philippians 3:10-11 where the Apostle Paul states his desire to "know Christ." The altar call that evening went out. It was plain and clear. The call was for anyone to come before God saying, "I don't want to know more *about* Christ, I want to *know* Christ better." As the music played and people sang, not one person made their way to the altar. Not...one. I thought to myself, "Really? Is there not *one* person in the room who would answer 'yes' to this call?" I will confess that I, too neglected the altar that night, and I will not attempt to offer an excuse for my own error. I should have been at the altar. I left that evening deeply disturbed in my spirit over the lack of response, and I would learn the next day that many others were just as disturbed.

I sought the Lord for an answer to this apathetic problem. He gave me a single word: "Dynasty." I was confused at first by this word and asked Him to elaborate on its meaning. God said, "Man-made, religious dynasties are not the Kingdom of God." You see, pride had taken over. The camp family had grown to place the camp as their first love. A big reset button needed to be pushed in our hearts, but how?

Fast forward one year. I had been asked to serve as Camp Pastor for the Family Camp which meant I would be preaching at all of the worship services. I knew God had asked me to prepare a message calling the camp to repent of what went wrong the previous summer. I wrestled with God and agonized over that sermon. What kind of reception and response could I possibly expect from such a direct message? Sometimes we are called to preach messages of an intense nature because of the intensity of the topic. This message, however, was intensely personal.

Near the end of the message I had a recording ready of Dr. Dwyer's altar call from the previous year. We played the two-minute segment. At the conclusion of the recording I asked the congregation how it could be that we could sit and hear such an impassioned plea and sit still in our seats. I reminded them that the altar was empty, that no living sacrifices were made there that night. I concluded the message with this statement: "I am going to issue a call tonight to repent much in the way Joshua called the Israelites to service and obedience. Choose this day what you will do, but as for me and my house, we will repent." With that I walked off the platform and made my way to the altar, the place I should have been one year earlier. I never looked up to see who came, but I'm told many joined me there and repented that night.

I heard one woman weeping deeply. She had recognized her own passivity toward the things of God. She later confessed to me, along with many others, that they did not even remember that altar call. The issues they repented of were the deadly mix of passivity and oblivion.

That message and the resulting repentance opened the doors for a deeply spiritual week. People's hearts had been stirred and stung by the power and presence of the Holy Spirit. We were attentive to what was spoken and how it affected our own hearts. God was so very good to us and met us there. One person wrote and sang a new song. Nearly every night there were testimonies to God's goodness and cleansing in their lives.

Do we display numbness to God even while present in church? Has our religion trumped true spirituality in Christ? We need to ask for, and humbly walk on, the ancient path of repentance.

Repentance is cleansing, but the process might hurt a little (or a lot).

Holiness, righteousness and peace, the fruit of repentance.

> "...but God disciplines us for our good, that we may share in his holiness. No discipline seems pleasant at the time, but painful. Later on, however, it produces a harvest of righteousness and peace for those who have been trained by it." (Hebrews 12:10b-11)

God's discipline leads to both holiness and a harvest of righteousness and peace. These are the blessed benefits of repentance. This is why repentance should be regularly encouraged in our churches and in our people. Repentance should be a topic embedded into our sermons and teaching. Why? Because of the harvest of righteousness, peace and holiness that is gathered at the end.

Repentance trains us to be more and more obedient as time goes on. The more we repent, the more joyful it becomes to obey. The more we repent, the more we recognize the harm that is done through our error. When we contrast the harm caused by sin to the harvest of holiness, righteousness and peace that comes through repentance, we will learn to be highly self-aware, and highly self responsive in repentance.

> "Even if I caused you sorrow by my letter, I do not regret it. Though I did regret it—I see that my letter hurt you, but only for a little while—yet now I am happy, not because you were made sorry, but because your sorrow led you to repentance. For you became

sorrowful as God intended and so were not harmed in any way by us. Godly sorrow brings repentance that leads to salvation and leaves no regret, but worldly sorrow brings death. See what this godly sorrow has produced in you: what earnestness, what eagerness to clear yourselves, what indignation, what alarm, what longing, what concern, what readiness to see justice done…" (2 Corinthians 7:8-11a)

Paul knew the benefits of "godly sorrow" that led the Corinthians to repentance. When is the last time we felt that godly sorrow?

If pride, passivity, error, idolatry or any other sin is present, then recognize that you are standing at the crossroads of sin and forgiveness. The crossroads calls us to an honest evaluation and presents an opportunity to repent and return to our loving Father with our whole hearts. Let us ask for the ancient path of holy repentance and may our feet be quick to walk that path with joy.

CHAPTER SIX

Spiritual Gifts

At the Crossroads of Need and Supply

J esus came to establish the Kingdom of God on earth. He accomplished His divine mission with no buildings, members, programs, doctrines, flow charts, 10-year plans or budgets. How did Jesus accomplish His mission without these things that we, as a church, find so vital and necessary today?

Jesus **proclaimed** *the gospel of the Kingdom of God*, and He **proved** His authenticity with *demonstrations of divine power*. Jesus took twelve men and taught them these same two principles of proclamation and power. He sent them out into their world with His message and His power. This is the only method ever endorsed by Christ and remains valid to this day.

Most churches today do not view Christianity through this lens. In organized religion, leadership is all about knowing who is in charge, who holds the power, and how things are controlled. In the Kingdom of God, however, Christ is the Head, the Holy Spirit gives us God's power, and we surrender control to serve our King and His mission. Today, having wandered light years from the ancient paths of proclamation and power, the church is weak, crippled, deformed, powerless, and on a steady decline into organizational extinction.

Think about it for a moment. The model by which most Western churches operate is *preaching + programs*, rather than *proclamation + power*. The church hires a paid professional or staff of professionals to create a religious organization that provides preaching and programs for their comfort and enjoyment. We also evaluate our churches by these metrics. We measure effectiveness not by the power of the Holy Spirit, but rather by location, budget, program, and charisma of the paid professional(s) and musicians. In all of this we have wandered off the ancient path of holiness and power onto a path of religious forms with no power. Take heart, we are not the first people in history to do this. There is also time to repent of our actions and return to the ancient path.

The religious leaders of Jesus' day were highly uncomfortable with the way He proclaimed His Father's message and demonstrated His Father's power. Matthew's gospel records the incredible story of how the Pharisees try to explain away Jesus' power, authority and authenticity.

> Then they brought him a demon-possessed man who was blind and mute, and Jesus healed him, so that he could both talk and see. All the people were astonished and said, "Could this be the Son of David?" But when the Pharisees heard this, they said, "It is only by Beelzebub, the prince of demons, that this fellow drives out demons." Jesus knew their thoughts and said to them, "Every kingdom divided against itself will be ruined, and every city or household divided against itself will not stand. If Satan drives out Satan, he is divided against himself. How then can his kingdom stand? And if I drive out demons by Beelzebub, by whom do your people drive them out? So then, they will be your judges. But if I drive out demons by the Spirit of God, then the kingdom of God has come upon you. Or again, how can anyone enter a strong man's house and carry off his possessions unless he first ties up the strong man? Then he can rob his house. He who is not with me is against me, and he who does not gather with me scatters. And so I tell you, every sin and blasphemy will be forgiven men, but the blasphemy against the Spirit will not be forgiven. Anyone who speaks a word against the Son of Man will be forgiven, but anyone who speaks against the Holy Spirit will not

be forgiven, either in this age or in the age to come. (Matthew 12:22-32)

The Pharisees, scrambling to maintain control and governance over the people, pronounced evil over the power of God by claiming that Jesus' power was of the devil! From that moment to today, evil people have been speaking evil over the power of God as a way to dismiss the Kingdom and maintain religious control. We, today, and yes even many in the denomination I serve, are guilty of this sin. Yes, to claim that the holiness and power of God is of the devil is actually a sin that will not be forgiven! How can I make such an observation as to say that we deny God's power in exchange for religious control? By the disdain with which we treat the supernatural gifts of the Holy Spirit. John Wesley understood this to be true in his day.

> "The grand reason why the miraculous gifts were so soon withdrawn was not only that faith and holiness were well-nigh lost, but that dry, formal, orthodox men began then to ridicule whatever gifts they had not themselves and to cry (against) them all as evil madness." -- (Ascension Feast of John and Charles Wesley, 1791 & 1788)

> "The cause of their decline (In the early Church) was not, as has been supposed, because there is no more need for [the gifts of the Spirit], "(Or) because all the world had become Christian". ... The real cause was: the love of many, of almost all Christians so called, was waxed cold; ... The real cause why the extraordinary gifts of the Holy Spirit were no longer to be found in the Christian Church [was that] the Christians were turned heathen again, and had only a dead form left. -- (Ascension Feast of John and Charles Wesley, 1791 & 1788)

The coldness of our love is drawing us away from God's power. We fear worship that is not decent or orderly. We figure that it's easier to eliminate the possibility of counterfeit gifts by squashing the movement of the Holy Spirit. God, deliver us from our error!

It's time for a rebellion.

With so many of the Spirit's marvelous gifts not in operation within His church; with our fears against them so heightened that we shun the thought of seeing them manifest in others, let alone ourselves; with our view of the gifts so skewed that we no longer see them as spiritual; with our current religious forms so ingrained within our DNA that we can't imagine what purpose the miraculous gifts could serve; it's time to launch a rebellion against our own fears and misunderstandings and allow Christ, who is knocking at our door, entrance into His own Church. It's time to expect to see the supernatural power of God manifest in our midst, and it's time to surrender control of the church back to Christ and the Holy Spirit.

So, here we are once again, at the crossroads. Will we continue down our current road of ignorance and/or resistance in regards to spiritual gifts and their purpose? Either we will continue down the road of spiritual weakness leading to our own destined organizational extinction, or we will be willing to reform, renew, recapture and restore the church as Christ intended. We must choose and we cannot choose both. If we choose His power, then it's time to launch a rebellion.

In order to launch a rebellion, we must "look" at the crossroads and have a clear understanding of the present condition. It is also necessary for us to have a clear understanding of the ancient path of power and proclamation. Power and proclamation are manifested in the church through the gifts given by the Holy Spirit. The power of Pentecost and the gifts given to the church to do the work of ministry demonstrate the Holy Spirit's miraculous power. However, many churches have remained so organizationally operational for decades without the gifts, that they no longer understand the purpose or function of the miraculous gifts within the body of Christ. We must be awakened to our location on an incorrect path leading to ineffectiveness as a church before we can ask for the ancient paths of power.

To each one ... manifestations ... for the common good.

"Now to each one the manifestation of the Spirit is given for the common good." (1 Corinthians 12:7)

Churches do well at sharing the message of salvation by grace, through faith. Yet, while we do well to tell people that God wants to save them, it is also important to instill within them the truth that God desires to sanctify them and mirror His holiness in them, fill them with His Holy Spirit, and give them gifts with which to serve the King in His Kingdom. Saved, sanctified, filled with the Spirit, and gifted by the Spirit for acts of service. Serving Christ is accomplished through the proclamation of the good news, and demonstrations of the Holy Spirit's power. As people grow in the grace and knowledge of our Lord Jesus, churches must encourage them to discover their calling and empowerment by the Spirit with which to serve the common good of the church and the world.

With all of this in mind, let's examine a model by which all of the gifts of the Spirit are present and accounted for. The following chart displays how all of the gifts work together in the body of Christ. It shows each gift as necessary and having a place. This is a complete and whole view of all of the spiritual gifts in operation. Take note of the five main categories of gifts and the primary gifting in each category. Spend some time observing and digesting the chart with all of its implications.

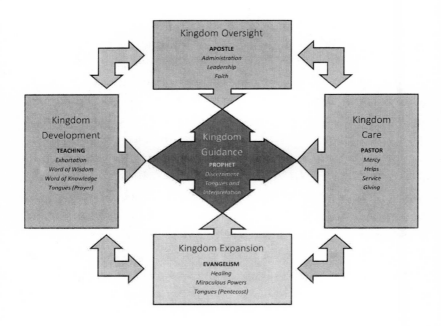

Kingdom Oversight

APOSTLE
Administration
Leadership
Faith

Kingdom
Development

TEACHING
Exhortation
Word of Wisdom
Word of Knowledge
Tongues (Prayer)

Kingdom
Guidance
PROPHET
Discernment
Tongues and
Interpretation

Kingdom
Care

PASTOR
Mercy
Helps
Service
Giving

Kingdom Expansion

EVANGELISM
Healing
Miraculous Powers
Tongues (Pentecost)

As you have examined this chart you may have questions, doubts and fears. There is really nothing to fear, and I believe any and all doubts can be addressed. The Holy Spirit's power is given as *gifts* to His children. We can, and should, look with expectation to the wonderful gifts God has for us. Taking this model of the gifts and their operation into account, let's now step back and discuss the things that have gone wrong over time and how we can launch a rebellion to set things right in the Body of Christ in regards to spiritual gifts.

Five points of error.

ONE: We've reduced the gifts to talents.

Organizations need talented, willing people to serve their structures. Churches have fallen into line with this worldly model and have begun conducting "talent surveys" under the guise of "spiritual gifts analysis tools." This first point of error is very deceptive. In the world, talented people are recruited to serve businesses requiring all kinds of specialized skills every day. Belief in Jesus is not required to be talented. Being filled with the Holy Spirit is not a pre-requisite for being smart. This is why it is possible to build religious organizations with spiritually empty, highly talented people.

Entertainment-based churches need marketing and PR people, clever orators, skilled musicians, computer and sound equipment operators, builders, maintenance people, and those gifted in programming for children. I would maintain that, with resources of talented people, it is entirely possible to build and maintain an organization structured around biblical themes and ideas. However, they are fully void of the power and presence of the Holy Spirit.

This reduction of gifts to talent explains the denial of the charismatic gifts of the Holy Spirit. "Our church is all about music, preaching and teaching. Who needs miracles or healing?"

TWO: We've extinguished the Spirit's fire.

The organizational and talent mindsets within many entertainment-based churches today extinguish the Spirit's fire. After Jesus ascended into heaven, His disciples followed His instructions by going to the upper room, and were obedient to wait on the Lord and pray for His power through the promised Holy Spirit. God answered and sent the Holy Spirit. The power fell on them like fire. God gave them unexpected manifestations of this power. He spoke through them in others' languages. He gave them a new life that was not able to be explained without His power and presence. He gave them power to heal the sick and cast out demons. This unexplainable, miraculous, powerful presence is the hallmark of the Spirit's fire.

Extinguishing the Spirit's fire happens the very moment we rely on our own strength, ideas and plans over that of God's. We also douse His fire when we deny the reality or truth of the gifts. When we begin to boast about what we've done, what we're doing, or what we plan to do, leaving God out of the equation, we've extinguished the Spirit's fire. When impatience with God drives us to act instead of waiting on Him, we've extinguished the Spirit's fire. When we speak out against gifts as unnecessary or bad, we extinguish the Spirit's fire. When the habitual resistance of the Spirit's fire becomes commonplace, we become spiritually dead even though we may be structurally and financially sound.

THREE: We've bought the enemy's lie that we're fine without the gifts.

The devil, the father of all lies, has deceived the church. What is this deception? It the erroneous belief that the supernatural gifts of God were only needed until the church had been established. The premise of this error is that once the canon of the New Testament was completed, and the world had been declared Christian by Emperor

Constantine, then the church had been established in the known world. Those who adhere to this teaching point to 1 Corinthians 13:10 as its fulfillment. The church would then be able to somehow run on its own without the supernatural power or gifts of the Holy Spirit.

Not only do I believe that teaching to be in error, but I also believe that nowhere in the scriptures is there the slightest hint that God would cease to pour out His power; nowhere is it stated that visions and dreams would cease prior to the return of Christ. The completeness spoken of in 1 Corinthians 13:10 is Christ's return and the arrival of the new heaven and new earth, not the compilation of the New Testament canon. Yes, when Christ returns to judge the living and the dead; when He hands the Kingdom over to the Father; then, and only then, will the demonstrations of the Spirit's power be no longer necessary. Until then, without the Spirit to empower us to testify to the life, ministry, death and resurrection of Christ, what hope do we have?

The enemy has convinced us to live with one hand tied behind our back, one eye covered over, and standing on one leg. At best we limp and crawl with limited vision because of the lack of supernatural power in our carnal organizations. Therefore, we need to be awakened to our crippled state and the deceptive voice of the devil.

FOUR: We've harmed brothers and sisters out of fear.

All the while we've been under the enemy's deception and living in fear of "those Pentecostal people," we have engaged in doing immense harm to those with genuine gifts of power from the Holy Spirit. We fear their display in our worship, we don't understand their purpose in the body, and so we completely disengage from attempting to understand. We've witnessed certain displays of the gifts and questioned their validity, fearing they are counterfeits. In the questioning, it has seemed easier to exert control rather than to discern. It is easier to say, "We don't do that here." It is far easier to exclude gifts than it is to disciple people and hold people accountable if something is spiritually amiss. Church, this is not the way Christ intended. In our need to control outcomes in worship, we harm those to whom the manifestation of the Holy Spirit has been given in ways we're uncomfortable with or do not seek to understand.

We must acknowledge the ways our behavior has created comfort for the controllers, yet harmed those under the weight of religious control. The church I serve is the Free Methodist Church. Where is the freedom in regards to gifts and manifestations of the Holy Spirit? Is the Spirit free to have His way?

FIVE: We've abandoned more than a few spiritual gifts.

To ignore the supernatural gifts of the Spirit places us in direct opposition to the holiness we preach and are determined to practice. To say we are holiness people, fully surrendered to God and dead to self, is negated when we begin placing God in a confined box. Yet this is exactly what has happened in many churches today. We speak declarations of the Holy Spirit's fullness, all the while diminishing His power by ignoring or outright denying demonstrations of His power.

Which gifts have we abandoned? Prophecy, miraculous powers, healing, tongues, interpretation of tongues, word of knowledge, and word of wisdom. These gifts are simply not possible in human strength and therefore can only be demonstrated with the infilling of the Holy Spirit.

To abandon any portion of God's power, based on how He has revealed Himself in the Scriptures, demonstrates our lack of surrender to God. The Acts 2 church was a holy, powerful church. They were devoted to the Apostle's teaching, the breaking of bread, fellowship and prayer. *Devoted.* Can we directly identify with them? Would the Apostle Paul, who said he spoke in tongues more than any of the Corinthians, be welcomed in our worship services? Would Peter and James be welcomed to heal a broken beggar at our gates? Would the prophet Agabus be given permission to prophesy and potentially interrupt our order of worship? God's power has never changed, but we have ceased seeking after it with our whole hearts.

Five points of rebellion.

Having recognized the five points of error, we stand at a crossroads. Will we walk in full submission to the Holy Spirit and open our hearts, minds and churches to Him, allowing Him to have His way? Or will we walk the path of fear and apprehension, keeping us from true freedom in the Spirit? If we are ready to ask for the ancient path, it becomes necessary to launch a rebellion against our fear and apprehension. Reform will come as the Holy Spirit guides if we are to open to a whole image of the Kingdom of God. These five points of rebellion will help us to deconstruct our flawed thinking and our old habits.

One: Repent.

Repentance is key. Admission of sin and wrongdoing, contrition of heart, and turning toward a new direction is the first step. We must not simply decide to try something new. This is not about, "Our way was okay, but we're willing to be flexible." Rather, our behavior calls for repentance. Repentance of sin and ignorance; repentance of control and management of God's church; repentance for putting out the Spirit's fire. Pastors, individuals and entire congregations must repent of this neglect. Repentance provides the prerequisite for the cleansing and openness of our hearts. In the posture of repentance God will meet us and fill us anew with His Spirit. With the gate of our hearts humbly open, we are free to receive much from Him.

Two: Wage war against fear.

Fear paralyzes, but God can set us free from our fears and the deception that caused them. "There is no fear in love. But perfect love drives out fear..." (1 John 4:18a) I understand the root of the fears, for I have experienced many of them myself. There was a time when I, too, was resistant to this kind of moving of the Spirit. Perhaps you've witnessed people who claimed to have a particular gift, and yet displayed no fruit in their lives that would indicate the presence of the Spirit. Maybe you've heard a false prophet who claimed, "The Lord says...", and was entirely wrong in regards to their message. Maybe you've seen faith healers perform their healing and you questioned the authenticity of their gifts. For every true display of God's power there are counterfeits. This has always been true. The solution to counterfeits is never fear. Fear keeps us from the fullness of God, while discernment, through wise rebuke of counterfeits, sets us free to seek the fullness of God.

Fears must be faced and dealt with. Confess your fear to God. Ask Him for wisdom. Seek wise teaching. Be open to exploring the scriptures for truth. Visit a congregation who worships in drastically different ways than you do. Face your fears and launch a rebellion to end them, for they are keeping you from the freedom God desires.

Three: Let God be God.

The only thing that will keep God from working in a human life is the human will. Holiness people believe in death to self and surrender of our will completely and entirely to His. If you believe this to be true, then any walls you've constructed in your heart and mind in regards to spiritual gifts must be tore down. To let God be God actually means, "Let your mind be open to a definition *of* God, *by* God, that could be radically different from the one you currently know." God's glory surpasses human understanding. He is beyond our grasp. If we would seek to know more of God, we can do so by accepting what He has already revealed about Himself. We must allow God to define Himself on His own terms through the biblical accounts.

Therefore we must rebel against our own stubborn will. Embrace God's great and wonderful gifts ... *all of them...* with complete acceptance. Do not lean on your own understanding and accept all of God's Word as truth. The truth will set you free.

Four: Relearn and reform our understanding of the gifts.

The fourth point of rebellion is against what has been planted in our minds through errant teaching, vacuuming the supernatural power from the gifts of the Spirit. Many believers have learned, through teaching and preaching, that churches can operate just fine without the supernatural gifts of the Holy Spirit. Because of this, we have much to unlearn and much to learn. Take a second look at the diagram presented earlier in the chapter. Ask yourself if you gave it full consideration when you first looked at it, or if you viewed it with resistance or skepticism. If you resisted it in any way, this time try to view it with acceptance through an open mind.

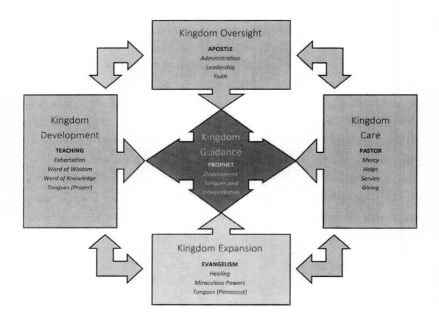

I had the opportunity to teach on spiritual gifts in my church and explore the themes of this chart in great detail. Our classes had some wonderful, challenging and thought-provoking discussion. God used those classes to tear down fears and open minds to new understanding. I believe we discovered some old abandoned paths, and determined to walk them.

Let's take a moment to point out seven key things found in this chart. An additional book would be needed to spend adequate time on a gift-by-gift analysis, but I believe these seven key points are the building blocks of changing our thinking and practice regarding spiritual gifts. The hope is to heighten our senses to many things we lack in our churches today because of wrong beliefs, and cause us to call on God, asking for the ancient path of His supernatural power.

1. **Every gift is represented and needed.** There is place for every gift and every gift has a place. The church is restored to wholeness and nothing is lacking. This should point out our neglect of many of the gifts. I believe the reason many gifts are neglected is that we lack understanding in terms of *why* the gift is needed and useful. God calls each manifestation a *gift*. He gives us gifts to do His work of ministry in the world. Just because we might misunderstand a gift does not mean the gift is useless, it just means we lack understanding and discernment. Wherever gifts are missing, so is true ministry effectiveness.

2. **The five-fold ministry is represented.** Paul's letter to the Ephesians says, *"It was he who gave some to be apostles, some to be prophets, some to be evangelists, and some to be pastors and teachers, to prepare God's people for works of service, so that the body of Christ may be built up until we all reach unity in the faith and in the knowledge of the Son of God and become mature, attaining to the whole measure of the fullness of Christ."* (Ephesians 4:11-13) Apostles, Prophets, Evangelists, Pastors and Teachers represent the five cornerstones of keeping the

body of Christ in harmony and interdependent operation. Respectively, the five key gifts lead the five key areas of need and ministry: Oversight (Apostle), Guidance (Prophet), Expansion (Evangelist), Care (Pastor) and Development (Teacher).

3. **The most misunderstood gift finds its home.** The gift of speaking in tongues finally has its proper place within the body. Three manifestations of this gift are found in scriptures, and each manifestation serves the body of Christ in a unique way. The first is proclaiming the gospel in a *known world language* when the speaker has never been taught the language (Acts 2:6). This manifestation of tongues has an evangelistic emphasis. God, who confused human language at the tower of Babel, reverses this confusion at Pentecost. The second manifestation is a prophetic message for the church from the Holy Spirit that requires interpretation (1 Corinthians 14:27-28). This gift is manifested within the context of the body of Christ when God has a message for the whole body. When a prophecy is delivered in a tongue, it requires interpretation so the body may respond to God's message. Finally, tongues is manifested as a language for prayer that edifies the spirit (1 Corinthians 14:14-15). This is a personal edification. Prayers in tongues erupt when the known language of the speaker becomes inadequate to express what is needed. The Holy Spirit comes upon us, praying and interceding through us when we are at a loss for words.

4. **There is no control, only interdependence.** When spiritual gifts are used for the common good, there is harmony and interdependence. Everyone in the body of Christ has two needs: The need to *serve* with their God-given gift, and the need to *be served* by others and their God-given gifts. When this functions properly, there is no room for domination, control, elitism or elevated importance of one person or gift

over another. Each gifted person beautifully serves every other gifted person within the church. The servant's heart guarantees mutual submission and love. There is no pride and no top-down hierarchy.

5. **Prophecy and discernment provide needed guidance.** Prophecy is the word of God coming (by way of the power of the Holy Spirit) through the servants of God, both foretelling future events (near or far) and forthrightly telling the wonders and works of God with the authority that comes from God. Prophets speak out of the voice given them through the Spirit's unction and provide God's messages for God's church. Prophets are thereby guides for the body of Christ. Prophets are needed because we cannot accomplish God's mission if we do not hear from our King. However, we know there are false prophets, so how do we know who they are? We need those gifted by God with discernment. Discernment is a witness from the Spirit of God in accord with the spirit of the believer, revealing both true and counterfeit spirituality. Those with discernment are like the marking pens used on currency to determine if they are counterfeits. Prophets are accountable to other prophets (1 Corinthians 14:32), and those gifted with discernment uncover the work of the enemy to deceive and derail the work of the church.

6. **Evangelism Regains its Power.** Today, Evangelists are defined as people who are highly educated and cunningly persuasive people trained in Christian apologetics. In other words, evangelists can easily "talk people into believing in Jesus." Evangelists have the answers to debate evolutionists, atheists, agnostics, and humanists. Consider, however, the impact supernatural power has to convince people of the reality of God. When the dead are raised, when the lame walk, when the blind see, people believe! (1 Corinthians 2:4-5) Evangelism also means that people reach across language and cultural barriers to proclaim the Gospel of Jesus. The gift

of tongues, as it was manifested on the day of Pentecost, is still needed today. Christianity today needs more than mere apologists. We need the power of God in our evangelism.

7. **All the Gifts are Spiritual.** Teaching, Helps, Giving, Leadership, Administration, and Service, all have carnal counterparts in the world's businesses and organizations. In the Kingdom of God, however, these gifts have both supernatural *purposes* and *power.* In the Kingdom of God, teachers impart Spiritual truth. In the Kingdom of God, helpers and those with gifts of service discern peoples' needs through the Spirit's unction and minister to the person based on that guidance. In the Kingdom of God, givers do so out of humble, godly love, not in hopes of receiving recognition. In the Kingdom of God, leaders and administrators seek the will of God for the people first and never lead out of selfish ambition. They seek God's guidance through the prophets and boldly show the way to the rest of the flock.

For many, this model will be strikingly different from what we have been previously taught. For others who have seen this type of model taught, you may still not see all of the gifts welcomed or in operation in your church. We need to be firmly committed to relearn and understand the power and purpose in each spiritual gift.

Five: Restore the lost practices of proclamation and power.

To recap from the start of this chapter, Jesus **proclaimed** *the gospel of the Kingdom of God,* and He **proved** His authenticity with *demonstrations of divine power.* Jesus took twelve men and taught them these same two principles of proclamation and power. He sent them out into their world with His message and His power. This is the only method ever endorsed by Christ and remains to this day. The call to our churches today is to reclaim proclamation over preaching in regards to sharing the good news, and power over persuasion or programs in regards to our evangelism.

At the crossroads, we stand and look over the current condition of our beloved church. Are we passive or powerful? Are we fearful or faithful? Is our power found in manifestations or management? We must decide if we will continue to extinguish the Spirit's fire or allow it to blaze in all its glory. It's time to launch a rebellion and overcome our fears and ignorance, blossoming into the full image of the church God had in mind from the foundations of the world.

CHAPTER SEVEN

Revival

At the Crossroads of Ordinary and Extraordinary

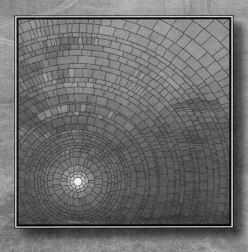

"I continue to dream and pray about a revival of holiness in our day that moves forth in mission and creates authentic community in which each person can be unleashed through the empowerment of the Spirit to fulfill God's creational intentions."

— John Wesley

re·viv·al noun \ri-ˈvī-vəl\

The growth of something or an increase in the activity of something after a long period of no growth or activity.

The dream for revival.

The reason this book exists is because God asked me to write it. I wish I could somehow get inside God's mind and find out why He asked *me* to write these words. In my mind, I know there are far more articulate and learned people than I. Along every step of the way during this writing, I have been confronted with my own shortcomings, yet I can't deny what I believe He's asked me to write. I also cannot deny the burning I feel deep inside for true revival to burst forth in our churches. I yearn for the true activity of the Kingdom of God to be reignited after a long period of inactivity.

Therefore, in response to God's call, I will share with you what I see from my point of view regarding the needed changes that must take place if we will see true revival in our churches. I understand many of you will read and receive this message as one man's editorial perspective. By *what I see* I mean a view of a preferred future for our churches that will require changes in modes, methods, attitudes, heart, determination, faith, love, and may require some paradigm shifts for us in terms of our praxis of ministry. I believe this vision is from God.

His vision came to me while at the camp, away on retreat. It was the second day. I had been reflecting on the view of the abandoned railroad tracks at the top of the hill, and the words God had spoken.

> "*The path has been abandoned, but the path is near.
> Rebuild the old path.*"

On this second day of retreat, God added one thought:

> "*Your forefathers blazed this path through the wilderness.*"

In thinking and pondering the themes of old paths, abandoned paths, rebuilding, blazing, etc., a thought came to me. I was reminded that God continually described Himself to the Israelites as the God of Abraham, Isaac and Jacob. He also called Himself the God of their forefathers. God has always described Himself in terms of relationships, events and encounters. We know Him through interactions that have been recorded in His Word. To see how God interacted with the Hebrew patriarchs, I began to study the accounts of Abraham, Isaac and Jacob found in Genesis. As I read the text all over again, God revealed something to me in Isaac's story that is the foundation of the vision. The vision found herein correlates to the path to true revival. Allow me to take you to that particular passage of scripture.

> Isaac planted crops in that land and the same year <u>reaped a hundredfold, because the LORD blessed him.</u> The man became rich, and his wealth continued to grow until <u>he became very wealthy</u>.

He had so many flocks and herds and servants that
<u>the Philistines envied him</u>. **So all the wells that his
father's servants had dug in the time of his father
Abraham, the Philistines stopped up, filling them
with earth.** Then Abimelech said to Isaac, "Move
away from us; you have become too powerful for us."
So Isaac moved away from there and encamped in
the Valley of Gerar and settled there. <u>Isaac reopened
the wells</u> that had been dug in the time of his father
Abraham, which the Philistines had stopped up
after Abraham died, and he gave them the same
names his father had given them. Isaac's servants
<u>dug in the valley and discovered a well of fresh water
there</u>. But the herdsmen of Gerar quarreled with
Isaac's herdsmen and said, "The water is ours!" So
he **named the well Esek, because they disputed
with him.** Then <u>they dug another well,</u> but **they
quarreled over that one also; so he named it
Sitnah.** He moved on from there <u>and dug another
well,</u> and no one quarreled over it. **He named it
Rehoboth, saying, "Now the LORD has given
us room and we will flourish in the land."** From
there he went up to Beersheba. (Genesis 26:12-23
(emphases mine))

In this passage we read of the envious Philistines stopping up
the wells of Abraham with earth and ceasing their flow of life-giving
water. Water is something most North Americans take for granted.
For the people of Isaac's day, water meant everything. If you had a
well, you were extremely wealthy and a single well could supply water
to an entire region. To stop-up a well with dirt would have indicated
a deep-seated hatred for the owner of the well. By today's standards,
stopping up a well could be equated to poisoning the water supply
of an entire city. Isaac moves into the territory where his father had

dug the wells and orders that they be dug up and given their original names. However, he doesn't stop there. Isaac orders that three more wells be dug. From the biblical account we learn that the first brings dispute, the second brings opposition, but the third is a symbol that they will flourish in the land. This story is a vision for revival for our churches; a vision of what was, what is, and what God intends to be.

The vision explained.

In the past, the great awakenings and revivals dug wells of deep spirituality flowing with living water from the Holy Spirit. These represent the original wells dug by Abraham. It seems, however, that God's children are never content to remain in the center of His will. Just like the children of Israel, who journeyed in and out of God's will, the church has also lived through times of both extreme darkness and disobedience as well as bright light and holiness. It is in the dark times, however, that the enemy came in and stopped up the wells of living water with lies and error. The enemies of the freely flowing water are pride, religious control, unconfessed sin, false teaching, false prophecy, and the list goes on. These stop up the wells of living water. The good news is, the water is still flowing beneath the surface! All that is required to regain access to the living water is to peel back the layers of the enemies' lies, removing the roadblocks to the flow of the Holy Spirit and drink from the living water.

Today, our churches stand on the very land where the water once flowed so freely, but the wells have been stopped up. It is time for us to begin to dig! We must recognize our dehydrated state, awaken our thirst and dig for water… the life-giving water of the Holy Spirit. We must thirst for revival more than anything else in our lives. We must return to the old abandoned paths of holiness, prayer and fasting. We must dig up the old wells, or risk extinction.

Beyond this first phase of revival lies the second phase of the vision. You see, there are also new wells to dig. God does not want to bless us with just our forefathers' spirituality. He wants to grant us additional blessings if we will seek Him with our whole hearts. That is what is meant by the next three wells Isaac has his servants dig in Genesis 26.

These new wells represent everything spoken of on the pages of this book. The new wells are representative of a fresh supply of holiness, a deeper heart for prayer, a longing to surrender our lives to God's control, an eager desire for every spiritual gift, a movement of humble repentance, and so much more. The new wells will unleash God's supernatural power. The new wells will gush with springs of living water. The new wells will unleash Pentecost-like power. The new wells are full of healing, vision, dreams, prophecy, and miracles, all pointing to Jesus as the central figure in all of human history, and ushering thousands upon countless thousands into His Kingdom of Light. The new wells will raise the dead, give sight to the blind and heal the cripple; all showing that the power of God has come to earth and His salvation is close at hand. The new wells will cast out demons, sending them into the abyss from which they came, through the authoritative name of Jesus. People will pray in the tongues of men and angels without ceasing. The new wells will awaken all that has been dormant for far too long. The Living Water found in the new wells will bring *revival*.

The vision also comes with a warning. I believe God is saying that as we attempt to dig the new wells, we will face the very same types of encounters that Isaac and his servants fell prey to. Because of these obstacles, the digging will require determination and persistence. We must not be moved from our determination to dig these wells if we want the revival God desires to give. With God's warning coming in advance, we can move in confidence, knowing He will be with us every step of the way. Though the devil would try to defeat God's plan and intentions, God's people, by His power, will prevail!

The first move of the Spirit will bring forth dispute.

As we move forward into the depths of our own hearts and the heart of God, and as we seek Him for revival, we can expect there to be dispute. Surprisingly, the arguments that provide the fodder for the dispute will come from both within and outside our churches. There will be those who do not understand why we are seeking something deeper. Quite honestly, these people will think that church-as-usual is just fine and should not be disrupted in any way. Others will say that you are taking these spiritual things far too seriously, and will actively work to bring your "fanaticism" into "moderation." Others will feel invalidated, as if their experience with God were being labeled by us as "substandard" when we call them to greater depths of spirituality. From outside, many will view us as fanatical or even dangerous.

One of the greatest sources of dispute is due to the fact that relativism has crept into our churches from the world in which we live. Within the church, any doctrine, any style, any method, any truth has become relative and individual. It seems we can hardly agree on anything. Because even people in many churches view truth as varied and individual, dispute will arise as we attempt to lead people to the living water.

Whatever form it takes, as we begin to dig the first well, representing seeking God for the first wave of revival, there will be dispute from inside and outside of the church. Of that, you can be sure. Do not fear the dispute. This dispute must take place because the idea of seeking God for revival will shine light on the current weak and lukewarm condition of the church and no one likes to be told they are wrong. Where there is denial, there is dispute.

The second move of the Spirit will bring forth opposition.

In an attempt to thoroughly discourage us from seeking God for true revival in our generation, there will come opposition. Yes, this is more fervent and active than dispute or argument. This is direct opposition that will seek to stop the digging and force us backwards into the lukewarm. Beyond simply voicing contrary opinions, the opposition will launch action to stop the efforts of those seeking revival. This will most likely come from within the church. Fearing change and seeing no need for the spiritual water sought out by the well diggers, people will confront, challenge, and place stumbling blocks in our way. They will demand that things are just fine the way they are. They will lean on the value of religious practice and traditions of men. They will seek to stop the move of God and seek to discourage the people who will be on their knees pleading with God for revival. In the midst of the discouragement, the temptation will be to give in, give up, and surrender to those who oppose us. Do not fear the opposition. The opposition must take place because once tangible changes are realized in our midst and stir our comfortable, predictable worship experiences to new places, people will oppose the change. No one likes to be proven wrong, so the opposition will largely be rooted in pride. God will use this difficult time to cleanse us of all pride.

The third move of the Spirit will allow us to flourish in the land.

Finally, the fresh living water of the Spirit will flow freely, for no one will dispute, nor oppose us. In light of the power God intends to pour out, no one will be able to refute the mighty hand of God moving among us. The third move of the Spirit will bring forth a great harvest of souls for the Kingdom of God and see the body of Christ minister, function and evangelize in the ways Christ has always intended. We will experience such beautiful interdependence, love, service and outreach into our world that everyone will know who "those Christian people" are. We will see God turn the enemy on himself and defeat him. There will be no more opposition, no more dispute, just freedom to live into our high calling to be a holy people, ministering in the name of Jesus to those in an unholy world.

That is the vision God has for His church if we are ready and willing to live into and up to the challenge and the call. It is time to ask for the ancient paths.

How to walk the holiness revival path.

All of the metaphoric language of paths and wells calls us to act… but how? If we are ready to act, if we have seen that we are standing at the crossroads, as we keenly observe and look over the current state of the church and find it to be dry, then we must know what to do in response. Corrective change is needed.

The path we must walk is very near, and is literally within the grasp of every person. Though only a few will choose this path, it is near and it is accessible to all. None are excluded. All are called. God is ready to meet us on the path.

So here is where I believe God is leading and how He is leading. Let's explore the themes of this book in terms of moving them from theory into practice. Pastors must be the first to embrace these truths and be willing to engage them in action. Without pastoral encouragement, congregations do not follow. The vision must be cast from a leader who has personally been changed and transformed. If there is a dedication to revival in the pastor, there will be a dedication to revival in the congregation. This is why pastors are the key. As pastors are challenged, transformed, and revived, individuals and congregations will follow. If leaders are not committed to revival, there is no chance for revival. If no one sounds a call, how can anyone respond?

Here, then, are the ways to get on the ancient paths and let the living waters flow. Perhaps you are now expecting the discussion to include sections titled "Five steps to unleashing healing" or "Three prayers God uses to send His Holy Spirit" or even "Fasting to get

God's attention." No, there are no self-help formulas or methods by which to trick God into giving us His power. You can, however, expect to be challenged to get off of the paths that have betrayed us, and onto the paths that will never betray us. You will also be encouraged to *walk* the paths. In other words, your daily life must embody the principles presented. The principles are designed to consecrate us as holy people, and center our hearts and souls on the Father, Christ Jesus and the Holy Spirit. The goal is humility, obedience, seeking, serving, praying, stirring, hungering and thirsting. It is also repenting of, correcting, abandoning and surrendering practices that have not served us well. God will guide you in both.

I, for one, am a *Free* Methodist who is determined to live in freedom and lead a church into the same freedom. Will you be set *free?* Are you ready to be led *to* God, that you may be fully led by God?

Start the rebellion.

Pastors and leaders first.

Fellow pastors, in order for a holy rebellion to be launched it must start with you. You must be willing to look over everything your church does from worship services to outreach events, from classes to programs. Everything must come under scrutiny for true Kingdom effectiveness and fruit. Furthermore, your own life must come under this same scrutiny. Do you want revival? Do you hunger for something more than the usual? Do you ever wonder where the supernatural power of God has gone? Are you so engaged in day-to-day ministry busyness that your own soul lacks in regards to deep relationship with God? Have you forgotten to mirror the leadership of the Apostle Paul, who led by example? Have you forgotten that we, as pastors, will be held to a higher standard before God?

Pastors, you must be willing to lead the charge against apathy. Had B.T. Roberts not stood against all of the apathy and ineffectiveness of the church in his day, there would be no Free Methodist Church. If you are not willing to stand against apathy and ineffectiveness in your own church today, and if you are not willing to admit the lack in your own congregation's spirituality because of personal pride, there will be no revival.

To actively launch the rebellion as a pastor requires both internal and external declarations that the battle has begun. You must use your knees to launch the inward battle against your own flesh and spirit, and then use the pulpit to proclaim the external call to the congregation. With your knees you will choose to personally surrender your life fully to God and with your voice you will call others to do the same. You must become the example, then lead out of that example. Your actions must be in perfect alignment with your words, and all must be aligned with Christ and His holiness.

Go back to chapter one and review the findings from the examination of your own life and the life and ministry of your church. Pastors, your commitment to do something about those areas of lukewarm and/or cold ministry and/or spirituality must become your top priority and cause within you a disruption in your soul, and the deepest heartbreak. Then, you must live and lead out of that heartbreak or revival will never come.

Frank Bartleman, one of the men who was a large part of the Azusa Street Mission and revival in Los Angeles in the early 1900's, wrote this in his diary:

> "It seems God can only get a man who has nothing but Heaven to live for to do the work for which a strong man is needed. I am glad to be used up in His service. I would rather wear out than rust out; and rather starve for God, if need be, than fatten for the devil."[3]

---

3   Bartleman, Frank (2011-09-21). Azusa Street: How Pentecost Came to Los Angeles (Kindle Locations 30-32). Jawbone Digital. Kindle Edition.

The Crossroads

Pastors, we must long to embody that spirit in our own lives. That is the kind of tenacity that will escape the numbness of apathy and willingly submit to anything God asks. To expect a revival in our churches without a revival in the pastor or leader is an exercise in futility. When a man or woman of God, charged with leading God's church, personally experiences and visibly displays the good fight of rebellion, the church will follow.

Individual and congregational implications.

Church, would you be willing to follow a passionate leader into the fires of revival? Would you be willing to follow the lead of your pastor and launch your own rebellion through soul-baring self-examination? Would you personally pray Psalm 139 and give God permission to boldly reveal the findings within your own soul? Are you ready to forsake the world and all its lures to be Christ's and Christ's alone?

Church, are you ready, not just individually, but collectively, to experience the power of God as a congregation like you've never experienced before? It might seem easy and appropriate to respond with an exuberant "Yes!" Before you do, ask yourself this question: "Are you ready to experience a radical change in the way you and your congregation worship and minister?"

Imagine gathering for worship in the kind of setting described from the Azusa St. Mission:

> "No subjects or sermons were announced ahead of time, and no special speakers for such an hour. No one knew what might be coming, what God would do. All was spontaneous, ordered of the Spirit. We wanted to hear from God, through whoever he might speak. We had no "respect of persons." The rich and educated were the same as the poor and ignorant,

and found a much harder death to die. We only recognized God. All were equal. No flesh might glory in His presence. He could not use the self-opinionated. Those were Holy Ghost meetings, led of the Lord. It had to start in poor surroundings, to keep out the selfish, human element. All came down in humility together, at His feet. They all looked alike, and had all things in common in that sense at least. The rafters were low, the tall must come down. By the time they got to 'Azusa' they were humbled, ready for the blessing. The fodder was thus placed for the lambs, not for giraffes. All could reach it."[4]

Church, are you ready to launch a rebellion against your own preferences to have church and/or do church the way in which you have become accustomed? Would you be willing to forsake your own human will in order to be subjected to the Spirit's will? Are you ready to step out of church as usual and into church is extraordinary? The rebellion that you must launch is to war against your own comfort and challenge your own expectations. We must deconstruct the old mindsets that everything is just okay to allow for something new. If your Pastors and leaders would lead you into green pastures and beside still waters, would you follow? Let the rebellion begin!

Together, pastors and churches must become dissatisfied with the status quo. It is that dissatisfaction that will drive the hunger for revival, and it is the hunger for revival that will drive the rebellion.

---

[4] Bartleman, Frank (2011-09-21). Azusa Street: How Pentecost Came to Los Angeles (Kindle Locations 902-909). Jawbone Digital. Kindle Edition.

Holiness that leads from death to self into life.

Pastors and leaders first.

A church will not naturally seek out holiness of life through death to self. Revival fires do not ignite into blaze spontaneously. They require pastors and leaders who have experienced the holiness of God like Moses did before the burning bush, but also experience the holy fire of the burning bush blazing in their own souls. Revival, in its truest sense of the word, requires holiness. This happens when we die to ourselves and our lives are cleansed of all unrighteousness and perfected in Christ's love. Our lives are stripped of all worldliness and take on the singular purpose of service to Christ. Our lives are obedient to His voice, available for His call, and subject to His authority. This message must be preached, but it must be lived-out first and foremost.

To be transported from spiritual death into spiritual life is the miracle of spiritual resurrection that comes before the bodily resurrection. Our earthly bodies are *in* the world, but not *of* the world because they have passed from death into life. Without this key transformational work in pastors, churches will never seek it or discover it for themselves.

Bold, fearless, spiritual, sanctified, consecrated, holy, passionate pastors are needed. Listen again, to the words of Frank Bartleman:

> "In the various crises that have occurred in the history of the church, men have come to the front who have manifested a holy recklessness that astonished their fellows. When Luther nailed his theses to the door of the cathedral at Wittenberg, cautious men were astonished at his audacity. When John Wesley ignored all church restrictions and religious propriety and preached in the fields and by-ways, men declared his reputation was ruined. So it has

been in all ages. When the religious condition of the times called for men who were willing to sacrifice all for Christ, the demand created the supply, and there have always been found a few who were willing to be regarded reckless for the Lord. An utter recklessness concerning men's opinions and other consequences is the only attitude that can meet the exigencies of the present times."[5]

The "religious conditions" of our time call for the self-mortification of all pastors and church leaders. I once had a pastor in our city tell me, "If you can hang on to the people you have, that is considered growth here." This defeatist attitude describes the prevailing tendency toward church survival, not true revival. Without true revival, we will most certainly become extinct, having been ineffective to reach our generation with the truth of power over sin and life of the soul.

Fellow shepherds, to begin the journey we must stop seeking anything other than Christ. Our own ideas have failed. We have tried every attractional church form our ingenuity can conjure and they have proven empty. Our methods may produce temporary attendance growth, but they do not produce true disciples of Jesus. People are attracted to entertaining services that package Christian themes in all sorts of culturally relevant facades, but we are ineffective in using opportunities to lead people to repentance, surrender, new birth and discipleship.

Think about it. In our efforts to be culturally relevant and hip, we have discarded pews and bought padded chairs; we have thrown out songbooks and bought video projectors; we have exchanged organs and pianos for guitars and keyboards. When it comes to preaching we ask people to consider what the Bible says instead of calling them to die at an altar. The end result of all our changes has produced a

5   Bartleman, Frank (2011-09-21). Azusa Street: How Pentecost Came to Los Angeles (Kindle Locations 710-716). Jawbone Digital. Kindle Edition.

version of the church that is still largely in decline, both in regards to numbers and in life transformation.

In attractional churches where the music and methods keep large numbers of people coming to services week after week, we must ask: what would happen to the spiritual well-being of those who are attracted if the attraction went away? Would people attend your services if there was no band, lights, videos or coffee? Death to self and the resulting life in Christ is the staying power for believers. All our current methods may go the way of other fads, but true holiness that comes from the death of the human will and surrender to God, is the only spiritual norm that is relevant to all humanity, and will never go out of style.

Pastors, we need to be reminded how the Apostle Paul taught Timothy.

> "Here is a trustworthy saying: If anyone sets his heart on being an overseer, he desires a noble task. Now the overseer must be above reproach, the husband of but one wife, temperate, self-controlled, respectable, hospitable, able to teach, not given to drunkenness, not violent but gentle, not quarrelsome, not a lover of money. He must manage his own family well and see that his children obey him with proper respect. (If anyone does not know how to manage his own family, how can he take care of God's church?) He must not be a recent convert, or he may become conceited and fall under the same judgment as the devil. He must also have a good reputation with outsiders, so that he will not fall into disgrace and into the devil's trap." (1 Timothy 3:1-7)

Holiness pastors are not soft on themselves. We somehow have grown numb or unaffected by the words in this passage. To live above reproach means that we must be unique or *other* in this world. The pastoral calling has deep implications of holiness that set us apart from any other type of occupation know to humanity.

Holiness pastors are not soft on sin. The wages of sin is death (Romans 6:23) and therefore pastors should never be soft on sin. Leading from personal holiness requires guiding people into the paths of holiness. To do so, all sin must be forsaken. Love people, but grieve the grip of sin over people's lives. Warn, direct, teach and preach against the grip and wages of sin. We must also teach the good news of Christ: that we can live free from the bondage of sin, the wages of sin, the grip of sin and the author of sin. Preach the freedom of holiness and the death of sin.

Holiness pastors are not soft on the world. Pastors, let me ask you: when was the last time something worldly or ungodly died in you at an altar? When was the last time you knelt or lay prostrate before God in submission? Does your church have an altar? Do you seek to blend into the world or be unique and somewhat outside the world? If your feet are on that ancient path of holiness, you will not walk on the world's streets.

Earlier in this book I told you my personal death story of sacrifice to God. My story is ongoing. My congregation knows my death story. They also know I have called them to the same death, that they might live fully in Christ. They know that in following Christ's example to be fully surrendered to the will of the Father, they will learn to trust God more and more. Does your congregation see the death example and hear the death call from you as their pastor and leader?

This comes with a price. Begin to dig this well and there will be dispute. Keep digging and there will be opposition. However, if you would seek God for revival, both personal and congregational, you must dig until you find living water. You must seek until you find. You must knock until heaven's door is opened. Pastors, the hole you dig will become a personal grave for any and all shreds of carnality left in you, and the springs of living water will fill your well and replace that which is dead and buried.

Individual and congregational implications.

Revival fires of holiness have profound implications for congregations.

Holiness brings the revival of true unity. When congregations have been cleansed of all sin and selfishness, and are on the ancient path to follow our Lord's instruction to consider others better than themselves, then the seeds of unity are planted and will grow. Holiness brings unity because personal preferences get set aside. Selfish preferences within congregations will always drive disagreement, and lead to divisiveness through power struggles. Imagine an entire congregation so dead to selfish ways and so alive to hear the Holy Spirit's voice that they begin to discern the Spirit in unity. In unity, the congregation moves to serve God as one body instead of a disconnected group of many people with differing motives, ideas and goals.

Church, how unified are you? Unity is far deeper than the ability to just get along with one another. Unity transcends being cordial to one another at church events. Unity in the Body of Christ is a connectedness of spirit, motive, mind, thought, and action. It is mutually submissive, contributing, serving and caring. Unity is needed in our churches. A revival of holiness will give birth to unity.

Holiness brings the revival of mutual soul-care. While most churches are great at combining resources to do *outreach* events together, holiness creates a bond between people in the Spirit where they excel in doing mutual *inreach*. By "inreach" I mean that believers let one another in on their personal spiritual transformation. Each person's life, experiences, struggles, joys and heartaches are handled with love and mutual concern. Everyone in the body grows while everyone is cared for. Everyone is transformed and all are dead to self.

Church, how close to this model are you? If your pastors and leaders called you to die to self, and modeled it with their own lives, would you give all for Jesus? Church, would you be willing to engage in transformational inreach with the same passion you engage in outreach?

This is one of the stepping stones on the ancient path of true revival. There is no substitute for this. Church, can you see that if we continue to do the things we have always done, we will continue to get the same ineffective results? Can you feel the winds of change blowing in the air? Do you hear the call of God? Holiness is the ancient path to revival.

Seek God for revival of the supernatural.

Pastors and leaders first.

Pastors and leaders, when is the last time something happened to you, near you, or through you, that could only be explained through the supernatural power of God? Has your role as a pastor become managerial or administrative? Is worship mostly programmed, predictable, and steady, or is it full of life, spontaneity, movement of the Spirit and Spirit-led order?

Consider this account from the days of the Azusa Street revival:

> "Someone might be speaking. Suddenly the Spirit would fall upon the congregation. God himself would give the altar call. Men would fall all over the house, like the slain in battle, or rush for the altar 'en masse', to seek God. The scene often resembled a forest of fallen trees. Such a scene cannot be imitated. I never saw an altar call given in those early days. God himself would call them. And the preacher knew when to quit. When He spoke we all obeyed. It seemed a fearful thing to hinder or grieve the Spirit. The whole place was steeped in prayer. God was in His holy temple. It was man to

keep silent. The Shekinah glory rested there. In fact
some claim to have seen the glory by night over the
building. I do not doubt it."[6]

Additionally, consider the way Jesus sent out the seventy-two and
the reason He sent them.

> After this the Lord appointed seventy-two others
> and sent them two by two ahead of him to every
> town and place where he was about to go. He told
> them, "The harvest is plentiful, but the workers are
> few. Ask the Lord of the harvest, therefore, to send
> out workers into his harvest field. Go! I am sending
> you out like lambs among wolves. Do not take a
> purse or bag or sandals; and do not greet anyone on
> the road. When you enter a house, first say, 'Peace
> to this house.' If a man of peace is there, your peace
> will rest on him; if not, it will return to you. Stay in
> that house, eating and drinking whatever they give
> you, for the worker deserves his wages. Do not move
> around from house to house. When you enter a town
> and are welcomed, eat what is set before you. Heal
> the sick who are there and tell them, 'The kingdom
> of God is near you.' But when you enter a town and
> are not welcomed, go into its streets and say, 'Even
> the dust of your town that sticks to our feet we wipe
> off against you. Yet be sure of this: The kingdom of
> God is near.' (Luke 10:1-11)

The Lord Jesus sent seventy-two disciples out with nothing but
God's authority to preach God's Kingdom message and demonstrate

6   Bartleman, Frank (2011-09-21). Azusa Street: How Pentecost Came
     to Los Angeles (Kindle Locations 922-926). Jawbone Digital. Kindle
     Edition.

God's supernatural power. That, dear friends, is the way the Kingdom of God works! No food provisions meant they would learn to receive the "daily bread" for which they had been taught to pray. No sandals meant they would feel every rock on every path, yet God would protect them. Jesus sent them out completely vulnerable like sheep among wolves. Healing the sick meant they would speak human words laced with God's authority and cause human flesh to be made whole! That is raw faith that trusts and expects God to display His supernatural power. That is the way Jesus taught His own disciples and has never endorsed an alternate method.

Pastors and leaders, do you know that your calling is to live daily in the supernatural reality of the Kingdom of God? Are you prepared to seek God for that power and use it when He calls you to? Are you willing to envision ministry that is Spirt-led, Spirit-powered and Spirit-supplied? Are you willing to exchange budgets and endowments for daily bread trust in God as your provider? Are you ready to be a faithful risk-taker, not putting God to the test but rather taking God at His Word to supply your every need?

Pastors and leaders, we cannot disciple people in ways we have not learned ourselves. The Kingdom of God is not the church facility we manage, or even the people we lead. The Kingdom of God is the reality of Christ as Ruler, reigning here on earth, from now through eternity! We serve Him in His Kingdom, and we are to do His Kingdom work. This work is not limited to acts of kindness or charity. These are good and commended by our Lord. However, we need to take up the supernatural authority Jesus gives us to push back the enemy in Christ's name. Jesus came and He preached the good news that the Kingdom of God was at hand. He then demonstrated the reality of the Kingdom through His mighty power in a variety of supernatural signs, healings, and miracles. When His disciples were sent out, they were given authority to do the same things and even greater things!

Revival comes when Pastors allow the Holy Spirit to lead. Pastors, when you lead in ways the Spirit directs and lead to places of

His choosing, revival comes. The only way this can happen is through much time spent in prayer, saturated in the Spirit's presence. Only you will know if you are leading out of your own convictions or the Spirit's convictions placed within you.

Revival comes when Pastors allow the Holy Spirit to manifest Himself. In the chapter on the missing power and presence of the Holy Spirit in our churches, I addressed the spiritual nature of the church, as well as the present hunger for the things of the Spirit. To experience true revival, there must be no resistance to, or attempts to extinguish the Spirit's fire. Pastoral permission is the key. Whatever you bind in the church and whatever you loose in the church will set the tone for the people. Addressing the hunger means that it must be satiated. Only the Holy Spirit, in the ways of His choosing, can do this. Extinguishing the Spirit's fire ensures revival will never come to your church.

Embracing the supernatural power of God through manifestations of the Holy Spirit also means we must embrace the spiritual gifts. To deny their working is to deny the Spirit Himself. To deny their power is to short-change or handcuff the church and cause it to attempt to function with an incomplete, maimed body. Pastors, you will never have all of the gifts. God intends to spread His riches throughout His church for the mutual benefit of all. However, people look to their leaders for guidance, approval and permission per se. When people are seeking entrance into the throne room of heaven, it is best not to stand in the doorway. Embrace, accept, seek, discover, and explore the wonderful, beautiful and powerful manifestations of the Holy Spirit. As one member of the body, working interdependently with others who are gifted in ways different from yourself, you must learn to trust the Spirit's movement and guidance in others in the body of Christ. To do this requires abandonment of all attempts to control the church and give the Holy Spirit full access.

Pastors, launch a rebellion against fear and move forward with joy into the revival fires of the power and presence of the Holy Spirit.

Individual and congregational implications.

Congregations who seek a corporate move of God and expect God to manifest Himself in the supernatural have profound impact in their communities. Revival comes with the wind of the Holy Spirit. Consider the means by which the Kingdom of God was tangibly demonstrated by Christ and His disciples: the sick were healed, the dead were raised, the broken were restored, the blind received their sight, the lame walked, the lepers were cleansed, the demon-possessed were delivered, and the good news was preached to the poor.

Take a moment, in light of this truth, and make a short mental list of everything you experience in your church. Include everything from outreach events and Christian education or small groups to the ways you personally serve the church or do tasks for the church. Finally, carefully inspect your church's worship services in your mind. How much of what Jesus demonstrated is regularly part of the life of your local church? How much of what Jesus demonstrated is *never* demonstrated in your church? Are you hungry for revival? Do you desire to see God move in supernatural ways, convincing people of the truth of God? Many churches are full of people who have been taught to lead services of worship and put together entertaining Christian events, but have not been discipled to live in the reality of the Kingdom of God. They have not been taught that the good news of the Kingdom comes complete with demonstrations of the Holy Spirit's power, proving its authenticity.

Perhaps you, like me, have never been told that this power is available to you. Well church, it is! God is not withholding His power, it is we who withhold our surrender and service to Him. If you knew that you could lay your hands on a sick person and they would be made whole, would you do it? If you knew that you could speak directly to a demon and command it to "go!" would you do it? Church, the most gracious, merciful thing you can do for a person is to engage your faith with God's power to see someone healed… restored… delivered!

Church, it is time to launch a rebellion against all fear and apathy and embrace the supernatural power of God!

Determine to touch heaven.

Pastors and leaders first.

All true revival is birthed from a movement of prayer that touches heaven.

I remember the day in January, 2011 that God confronted me with a reality of my life that needed attention. He said to me, "Brett, you are a man who prays, but you are not a man of prayer." God's words confronted my personal prayer life: that it was weak, shallow, and largely ineffective. Because my prayer life was weak, my relationship with the Father was suffering. When God called me to pray more, He was basically inviting me to a fuller relationship with Him.

> *Busy pastors "work hard" ... Pastors*
> *with thirsty souls "pray hard."*

Pastors, are you men and women of prayer, or do you just occasionally pray? Is prayer the thing you do when there's extra time, or do you pray because, without it, your relationship with the Father will suffer? Do you *love* to pray and *live* to pray, or do you *have* to pray? Is your prayer conversational and alive, or rote and mechanical? Do you anticipate your time with the Father like a child longing for the presence and attention of a loving parent, or do you remember that you have to schedule God in for a time of prayer, wondering how it will fit into your busy schedule.

When it comes to prayer, the truth is undeniable that congregations will not rise above the practices exemplified by their pastors. Congregations will see prayer as a life-giving priority if they see their pastor as a person of prayer. That being said, how dedicated are your people to prayer? Does your church place a high priority on prayer (both individual and corporate prayer)? Do you preach and teach on the importance of prayer? The strength or weakness of your congregation's prayer life may be directly tied to your own personal prayer life and your dedication to corporate prayer (or lack thereof).

Pastors, if you and I don't have time to pray then we are likely believing that the work of ministry can carry on in our own strength. If we are not seeking God for His voice and answers to the impossible work of ministry, then we are missing out on abundant blessings through answers to prayer.

The determination we must have as shepherds of God's church is to regularly touch heaven in prayer. This will happen when we launch a rebellion against activity of all kinds. We must set aside meetings with people for meetings with God. We must determine not to engage our own ingenuity and strength before seeking God. We must lead out of our relationship with God.

> Now Moses used to take a tent and pitch it outside the camp some distance away, calling it the "tent of meeting." Anyone inquiring of the LORD would go to the tent of meeting outside the camp. And whenever Moses went out to the tent, all the people rose and stood at the entrances to their tents, watching Moses until he entered the tent. As Moses went into the tent, the pillar of cloud would come down and stay at the entrance, while the LORD spoke with Moses. Whenever the people saw the pillar of cloud standing at the entrance to the tent, they all stood and worshiped, each at the entrance to his tent. The LORD would speak to Moses face to face, as a man speaks with his friend. Then Moses would return to the camp, but his young aide Joshua son of Nun did not leave the tent. Moses said to

the LORD, "You have been telling me, 'Lead these people,' but you have not let me know whom you will send with me. You have said, 'I know you by name and you have found favor with me.' If you are pleased with me, teach me your ways so I may know you and continue to find favor with you. Remember that this nation is your people." The LORD replied, "My Presence will go with you, and I will give you rest." (Exodus 33:7-14)

Pastors, in prayer we must come to God with the very same heart as Moses. We, too, must seek God and ask to be taught God's ways. Why did Moses ask for these things? So he could *lead the people.* Why do pastors need to pray? So we can lead God's church to accomplish God's purpose by doing God's will in exact alignment with God's plans. It really is that simple, and yet that profound. If pastors are men and women of prayer, seeking God so they can lead, then the results will lead to carrying out God's purposes and plans on earth.

This is crucial for revival. Consider the town, village, city or region where you pastor and serve. Is there brokenness there? How deep is the brokenness? In our city, Jamestown, NY, there is a profound drug problem. We seek God in prayer regularly to deliver our city and its people from the bondage of drug addiction. I'm convinced that God is waiting for us to be truly and earnestly grieved to the point of tears for our city. Jesus wept over Jerusalem, and I believe that following Jesus means our hearts should break for the regions we serve. Prayer that is birthed from godly heartbreak will open the gates to revival.

When pastors are men and women of prayer, they may encounter dispute, or even opposition from within the church. Prayer is not a popular program. Church members pray in times of tragedy, but they do not naturally migrate to deep prayer. They need to be led there, and that responsibility falls on the pastor.

Individual and Congregational implications.

Church congregations need pastors who are men and women of prayer to lead them to be people of prayer. Think in terms of the upper room as described in Acts 1.

> "When they arrived, they went upstairs to the room where they were staying. Those present were Peter, John, James and Andrew; Philip and Thomas, Bartholomew and Matthew; James son of Alphaeus and Simon the Zealot, and Judas son of James. They all joined together constantly in prayer, along with the women and Mary the mother of Jesus, and with his brothers." (Acts 1:13-14)

"They all joined together constantly in prayer." They *all*. No one was left out of this continued prayer meeting. Everyone joined. Everyone had a passion for it and everyone saw the need for it. Everyone obeyed Jesus' command to return to Jerusalem and wait. And they did this through prayer. *Constantly.* There were no interruptions and no set stop times. They prayed. How does a church join together in prayer? How does a congregation capture such a vision? Church, we must launch a rebellion against the notion that prayer is "optional."

Have you ever attended a concert of prayer? I have. The idea is that many people gather for one purpose and that is to pray. However, I'm not sure the name adequately reflects the intended purpose. What do I mean by that? Well, people attend concerts every day. They sit in rows and listen to the music or performance by whoever is on stage. At the conclusion, people applaud in proportion to their approval of the entertainment, then return home. I have been to many concert of prayer events where the attendees mostly sit in rows and listen to the prayers of the leader at the front. At these concerts of prayer, usually there are topics presented in a prescribed order then one leader at the front of the room prays. Now, I'm not necessarily suggesting this form is bad. However, I have witnessed a different type of prayer gathering that is rich and beautiful. Rather than a concert of prayer, I would liken it to choir of prayer.

In a choir everyone sings. In a choir of prayer everyone lifts their voice and contributes to the "concert." In a choir, God's children are the participants while God is the audience. In a choir, everyone brings a different voice and contributes to the choir in a different way. In a choir of prayer, all voices contribute to the whole. In a choir of prayer, the contributions make different sounds but the harmony is incredible.

> "Again I say unto you, that if two of you shall agree
> on earth as touching any thing that they shall ask,
> it shall be done for them of my Father which is in
> heaven." (Matthew 18:19 KJV)

As Jesus instructs us in what prayer can do, He even shows us the power of the duet. Even in the duet of two, they both touch, they both agree, they both ask. There is something beautiful that happens in heaven when God's people sing together in prayer! In the concert, there are many passive observers, but in the choir, there are many passionate participants.

Today, the traditional church choir (that is, the musical kind) is becoming less and less commonplace. Perhaps this is a good thing. Perhaps the kind of choirs our Lord is looking for are the kind where everyone prays, everyone engages their heart in prayer, everyone lifts their voice in prayer, and no one is a passive observer. No one would argue against "more prayer." All true revival begins with a choir of prayer. One may be praying for revival, but what happens when two, three or more begin to pray for this same thing?

Dear church, become a living, breathing choir of prayer. Don't worry about who is the soloist, who can sing the highest or lowest, or who has the prettiest voice. In this kind of choir, that is not important.

Brett Heintzman

Everyone can contribute. Everyone should contribute. God is waiting for us to touch, ask, and agree in prayer for the revival that will change us and the world around us. Do you desperately seek God to bring revival? Pray. Pray more. Pray deeper. Pray without ceasing.

Live in a rhythm of repentance.

Pastors and leaders set the tone and churches follow.

All revival begins with a season of repentance. Pastors, without your willingness to repent of something in your life or church that is worthy of repentance, then your congregation will see no need to repent either.

In August, 2010 it was suggested to me that a healing service be held at our church. In my very short time at the church, I had discovered that there had been past troubles. The church had gone through a very rough time and the people were largely discouraged. To add to the discouragement, I had learned of rumors concerning the church's past. Having a lengthy history of nearly 145 years, the church had been through seasons of trouble before. The details are not necessary but I had discovered that much of the trouble from the past had been swept under the proverbial carpet and left in the past. I had never encountered something like this before. How was I to lead a service of healing in the present day for things in the past? I asked God to help me.

I had many questions going into the Sunday evening service. Why would we in the present day need to repent of anything in the past? We didn't commit the sins of our fathers. What could hope to be accomplished by confronting the hurt of the past? As I prepared for that evening, God gave me two passages of scripture. The first passage was from the fifth chapter of John's gospel. The story is the familiar account of the invalid man at the pool of Bethesda. He is unable to get into the waters when they are stirred to receive his

148

healing. He is discouraged and *stuck*. He has no hope. Here is the story:

> One who was there had been an invalid for thirty-eight years. When Jesus saw him lying there and learned that he had been in this condition for a long time, he asked him, "Do you want to get well?" "Sir," the invalid replied, "I have no one to help me into the pool when the water is stirred. While I am trying to get in, someone else goes down ahead of me." Then Jesus said to him, "Get up! Pick up your mat and walk." At once the man was cured; he picked up his mat and walked. (John 5:5-9a)

The second scriptural account God gave to me was from Daniel, chapter nine. Daniel comes before God in prayer at the completion of seventy years of Babylonian exile for the people of Israel. His heart is open and ready to confess "the sin of his people." Hear the account and prayer of Daniel:

> So I turned to the Lord God and pleaded with him in prayer and petition, in fasting, and in sackcloth and ashes. I prayed to the LORD my God and confessed: "O Lord, the great and awesome God, who keeps his covenant of love with all who love him and obey his commands, we have sinned and done wrong. We have been wicked and have rebelled; we have turned away from your commands and laws. We have not listened to your servants the prophets, who spoke in your name to our kings, our princes and our fathers, and to all the people of the land." (Daniel 9:3-6)

> "Now, our God, hear the prayers and petitions of your servant. For your sake, O Lord, look with favor

---

on your desolate sanctuary. Give ear, O God, and hear; open your eyes and see the desolation of the city that bears your Name. We do not make requests of you because we are righteous, but because of your great mercy. O Lord, listen! O Lord, forgive! O Lord, hear and act! For your sake, O my God, do not delay, because your city and your people bear your Name." (Daniel 9:17-19)

To be perfectly honest, I didn't want to preach on these two scriptures that evening. I kept looking for another way and/or another word. There was no other way. This was the path to healing that God had chosen for us. When I expressed my turmoil and struggle with these passages of scripture to a brother in our congregation, he simply said, "And you're not being obedient *why?*" I entered the service with a timid, yet determined resolve, waiting to see what God would do.

I had no idea that He wanted to change *me* as a pastor, leader and person during the service. The time came to bring these words from God. I encouraged the congregation by telling them that God wanted to heal and deliver us. However, that would require humility and repentance on our part. If we were in exile due to the sin of our fathers, it was right and appropriate for us to repent. We, like Daniel, could pray and confess, cry out and repent. We could put on the sackcloth and ashes of mourners and grieve what had been lost. We could call on God and seek His mercy "for such a time as this." In the same way, we needed to open our ears and hear Jesus asking us, "Do you want to get well?" I told the church that if our answer was "yes," then we would need to walk in new ways beyond the point of healing. Our status would change from "invalid beggar" or "victim" to "whole" and "victorious." God was willing, ready and able to make us whole... but did *we* want to get well?

We entered a time of prayer. People began to pour out their hearts to God. When hearts are poured out in repentance, the penned-up junk of the past gets swept away. I found myself soon kneeling at

150

the altar. As people were praying, God said to me, "That's not low enough." I knew what God meant. My physical posture was to mimic the posture of my heart in repentance. I crouched down further so that my forehead was resting on the altar rail. God said, "That's not low enough." This time I crouched down even lower. I was tucked into a fetal position still on my knees and I continued in prayer. A short time later God said, "That's not low enough." This time there was nowhere else to go. For the first time in my life, I lay prostrate on the floor with my face in the carpet. People in the congregation were weeping and crying out to God. Hearts were being poured out to God in beautiful repentance.

Our church was made "well" that night. God honored our prayer. The spiritual forces of darkness that had oppressed our church were gone. We had been gloriously delivered! A fellow colleague came to the church about a week after our healing service. He asked me what had changed about the church. He said, "It's different here somehow. It's brighter." He was not suggesting that we had installed additional light fixtures. The darkness had fled through our repentance. We cried out to God and He set us free! From that moment, we began to enter a season of "increase" that has not stopped yet. Increase in faith, healing, deliverance, salvation, spiritual formation, and yes, even giving and attendance. Looking back these past four years, I highly doubt that the increase we have witnessed in our church could have been possible without that key step of humble repentance before God. I have since learned that repentance is something that should be a recurring theme in our ministry. There are many occasions when any pastor or church should repent.

- When we've disobeyed God's leading or commands.
- When we've acted in ignorance.
- When there has been sin in the camp.
- When there is moral failure.
- When we've grown complacent or lukewarm.
- When we've not trusted God.

The questions are before us. Do we need to repent of anything at this time? Do we need to repent of anything in the past? Do we want to get well? Do we hunger and thirst for revival? Do we desire to see a reawakening of holiness in our day that is unmatched by anything we have previously witnessed?

Lighting the Fires of Revival

There is no linear progression or specific formula guaranteed to bring revival to you or your church. Rather, there is a perfect storm of behaviors that, when present in the lives of pastors and churches, create the perfect conditions for God to birth revival. Revival is not a something that is to be sought, but rather an inevitable byproduct of the true holiness church.

- A church that continually wars and rebels against all apathy and stagnation will experience revival.
- A church that dies to itself so that it might live into Christ, and is constantly seeking more of Christ and less of themselves, will experience revival.
- A church that releases their hands of all control and allows the Holy Spirit to manifest Himself in supernatural ways will experience revival.
- A church that, with fully engaged hearts, regularly touches heaven in prayer, and fasts in response to the call of God, will experience revival.
- A church that takes up the authority of Christ to push back the darkness in Jesus' name will experience revival.
- A church that mutually benefits one another with their Spirit-given gifts, and embraces the reality and function of all the gifts, will experience revival.

♦ A church that is ready to repent when needed and has experienced the wholeness that comes from pouring out their hearts in repentance before God will experience revival.

All of these truths are to be practiced in our churches in an ongoing and overlapping fashion. Every theme is a continuum of activity, not a destination. They are desired conditions of the heart, not spiritual accomplishments.

This, dear friends, is the ancient path of holiness. This is the abandoned path that needs to be rebuilt. This is the path that our spiritual forefathers blazed through the wilderness. The ancient path leads to revival. There are likely paths your church is walking that should be abandoned in favor of this better way. It is never too late to begin walking the ancient paths. You and your church are literally one choice away from revival. Like the Israelites of old, our choice happens at the crossroads.

Epilogue

As the Israelites stood at the crossroads in the days of Jeremiah the prophet, they had a choice to make. God offered His people the opportunity to reconsider the errant path they had been taking and ask for the ancient paths previously given to them, leading to life. However, the last part of Jeremiah's pronouncement of the Lord's Words revealed the state of stubbornness in their hearts.

> "But you said, 'We will not walk in it.'" (Jeremiah 6:16b)

How can someone, *anyone*, turn down the offer of life extended to them by the Living God? Sadly, God's offer for life, abundant life, and His power and authority are turned down every day. It would seem logical to say that people who have never heard the gospel, or who continue to live in the grip of sin, turn their backs on God regularly. To put things in perspective, however, it must be remembered that Jeremiah's words were given to the Children of Israel... God's chosen people. The crossroads was a dangerous place for the Israelites. There was still time to change direction and return to the Lord's ways but they responded with their choice and told God "No!"

How sad would it be for your church or mine to hear the call of God to return to Him with all our hearts and respond with a resounding "No!"

> "But I tell you, Do not swear at all: either by heaven, for it is God's throne; or by the earth, for it is his footstool; or by Jerusalem, for it is the city of the Great King. And do not swear by your head, for you cannot make even one hair white or black. Simply let your 'Yes' be 'Yes,' and your 'No,' 'No'; anything beyond this comes from the evil one." (Matthew 5:34-37)

Jesus' point in this beautiful passage from the Sermon on the Mount is that the substance of every oath you take is found in your actions. Oaths are full of cheap words that only gain their value when actions align perfectly with them. Therefore, only say yes or no when you are prepared to demonstrate your words with your actions. In the words of Jesus, "Anything beyond this comes from the evil one."

Perhaps you have been tracking with the thoughts presented in this book and might be willing to take a verbal oath of agreement with them. However, the question remains, "Are you ready to take an **active** oath?" Are you ready to give your yes and amen at the crossroads? It's one thing to say we want the Holy Spirit to be in control, it's another thing to give up our own control. It's one thing to say we believe in entire sanctification, it's another thing to die to ourselves. It's one thing to say we will pray more, it's another thing to give up things on our schedule to actually pray more. It's one thing to say we believe in all of the gifts of the Spirit. It's another thing to anticipate and eagerly desire the manifestations of the Spirit in all His fullness. It's one thing to say we need revival, it's another thing to be an agent of revival. It's one thing to say we know God is supernatural, it's another thing to expect the supernatural power of God to be manifested in His people.

As we begin to conclude our time together through this writing, I invite you to return with me to the words God gave me that prompted this entire message:

> *"The path has been abandoned, but the path is near.*
> *Rebuild the old path."*

To walk in the ancient paths is to actively engage in the ministry that was originally given to the church through our Lord Jesus. This ministry He handed down to us has never changed. Hence, it is the ancient path. Our present-day actions have shown clearly that many have abandoned this old path. Christ's ministry is centered on the redemption and restoration of people. His ministry was always announced through the proclamation of the Kingdom of God (preaching), and accompanied by tangible demonstrations of the Kingdom through healing, forgiveness, deliverance and restoration (power). We as a church must examine the path we are walking. Is the current path on which you and your church travel the path of God's choosing, or a man-made, highly organized, man-controlled, powerless path?

Hear Jesus describe the ministry given to Him, and hear how he sends out His disciples to do the very same ministry.

> "The Spirit of the Lord is on me, because he has anointed me to preach good news to the poor. He has sent me to proclaim freedom for the prisoners and recovery of sight for the blind, to release the oppressed, to proclaim the year of the Lord's favor." (Luke 4:18-19)

As you go, preach this message: 'The kingdom of heaven is near.' Heal the sick, raise the dead, cleanse those who have leprosy, drive out demons. Freely you have received, freely give. (Matthew 10:7-8)

And these signs will accompany those who believe: In my name they will drive out demons; they will speak in new tongues; they will pick up snakes with their hands; and when they drink deadly poison, it will not hurt them at all; they will place their hands on sick people, and they will get well." (Mark 16:17-18)

Heal the sick who are there and tell them, 'The kingdom of God is near you.' (Luke 10:9)

Brothers and sisters in Christ: the power and authority of God is given to you through our Lord to push back the darkness and reveal the light of the Kingdom of God to the world. God's power is not for us to create nicer looking buildings and produce more creatively appealing worship services. It is not given to craft oratorical masterpieces for sermons. The power of God is given to the church for the same reason it was given to Jesus... to tangibly show that the Kingdom of God is at hand. Jesus showed His disciples that path and then showed them how to walk in that path. He provided all the power and authority needed to walk that path.

Like an old set of seemingly useless railroad tracks, the old path is very near. We are not far from the path. For many of us, we already speak of many of these concepts, but we fail to act on them. The Bible is full of prophetic voices calling the people of God to abandon their futility and return to God's ways and His power. Jeremiah's call to the Israelites was clear. Equally clear was their rejection of that prophetic word. Let us not make that same mistake in our generation.

Today, our Lord is saying the same thing to us that He said to the children of Israel years ago: "Stand at the crossroads and look; ask for the ancient paths, ask where the good way is, and walk in it, and you will find rest for your souls."

Will we say in our generation, "Yes, Lord! We *will* walk in it."? Amen… may it be so.

CPSIA information can be obtained at www.ICGtesting.com
Printed in the USA
BVOW07s1242260115

384982BV00001B/1/P

9 781490 866628